3rd Edition, 1984

Dedicated to everyone who has offered their sup-
port during my shooting career and helped make
this book possible so others might benefit and en-
joy their shooting endeavors.

CONTENTS

Introduction

BY Massad Ayoob

It gives me unique pleasure to write the foreword for John Shaw's book, because I feel that the big Tennessean has carved a unique niche for himself in the history of competitive handgunning.

I first met John in the late 1970's, when we were both pretty much "journeymen" on the so-called professional handgun competition circuit. If shooting had been golf, John and I would have been the sort of players who make a living on the tour, but never take the Masters.

Perhaps my fondest memory of John is at the Second Chance event in 1979. Because the year before I had finished fourth and he fifth, we figured we were suitably matched for the two-man team event. We finished in the top five teams, in a four-way tie for fourth slot. In a freezing drizzle, sponsor Richard Davis announced that the tied teams had their choice of shooting off, winner take all, or splitting the prize money.

I recall that year fondly, for two reasons: When everyone else was happy to take the split and go home, my partner John was yelling, "Hell, no, we wanna *shootoff*!" The second reason is that '79 at Second Chance was the last year I ever beat John in a tournament.

That was the year John decided he wasn't going to be an also-ran anymore; he was going to be leader of the pack. What followed was a deep period of soul-searching, and, ultimately, a self-improvement program that was 100% a commitment to personal excellence.

To understand the meaning that John Shaw's experience has to the average person reading this book, one must understand the composition of the typical champion in the practical pistol game. Mickey Fowler was already a champion athlete when he picked up the gun. Ray Chapman and Ross Seyfried, America's two World Champions, were all but unbeatable from the beginning of their careers, as if their Pachmayr .45s were magic swords like Excalibur that they had drawn from the rock with annointed hands.

Shaw was different. He had never been an athlete or a super-competitor before . . . but he rose from the middle of the pack to set the prize records at Second Chance and to claim an unprecedented two consecutive wins at the American IPSC National Championships.

In the years that followed the emergence of "the New John

Shaw" in 1979, we've seen a trend in practical pistol shooting toward the Clark "Bowling Pin Gun" he popularized, and manufacturers have been beating down his door for product endorsements. Still on the lighter side of thirty, in a game where many of the great champions peak between thirty and fifty, I'm confident that John will continue to write practical pistol history.

The key thing to remember as you read this book is that John wasn't your basic gifted athlete or "born winner." Nor does he owe his skill to the tutelage of some handgun guru; he is almost entirely self-taught.

No, the John Shaw Story is the story of a man who, by sheer will and determination, coupled with the techniques described in this book, blasted his way to the top the hard way. In the last analysis, the thing you should understand when you read every word in this book is that everything John Shaw did to become a great champion is something *you* can do . . . because John Shaw is the champion *you* can be, if you take his advice to heart.

Massad F. Ayoob
Concord, NH 03301
May, 1982

Best know as an award-winning gun writer for *American Handgunner, Guns, Combat Handguns, Gun World,* and numerous police publications, Massad Ayoob is also a national record-setting competition combat shooter who has placed in the top 5 at Second Chance, the top 15 at the Bianchi Cup, and held State and Regional Championships. He has followed John Shaw's career "in the arena", as both a fellow competitor and a chronicler of the sport, since 1978. He privately refers to Shaw as "one of the most likeable contestants on the competition circuit, and one of the most helpful to his fellow shooters."

What is Practical Shooting?

Forget everything else you've heard about the mysteries of shooting—shooting is easy.

The purpose of YOU CAN'T MISS is to help teach you, the reader, my most recently developed techniques for combat shooting—techniques that work. I hope to correct some of the misconceptions and misinformation about practical shooting, as well as providing the necessary information for you to improve your shooting skills for either competition or self-defense. There's nothing mysterious about good shooting. It's a combination of the basic modern techniques and rigorous practice. If you follow the recommendations outlined in this book, I believe you can't miss—you will get better. First, though, remember the basic idea behind my techniques:

Shooting is *easy*.

I know that's hard to believe. At times, really top-notch shooting, expecially pistol shooting, sometimes seems to border on magic. Watching top trap shooters, police PPC experts, or combat champions display their skills is a lesson in humility—how *did* they get that good? Could *I* ever get that good?

That was the first thought in my mind when I made the decision to go from casual plinker to professional competitor. Like most kids growing up in the South, I was passingly familiar with handguns. I spent much of my time relaxing from the rigors of college life shooting tin cans and cottonmouth snakes with a .22 automatic, and among my friends I was known as a pretty good shot.

When I made the commitment to enter competitive pistol shooting, I discovered that my hard-earned plinking skills didn't amount to much at all. I really didn't know *anything* about what it took to be a good shot. But I had made a commitment to myself: I would become a champion, and I would teach myself how to do it.

I think I made every mistake possible. Techniques that I thought were great didn't hold up in matches. Things I had read about pistol shooting, the *right* way to shoot a pistol, just didn't seem to work for me. I could learn to do things *correctly*, but they just didn't translate into good shooting.

It slowly dawned on me was that there was some missing element, some key to good shooting that I couldn't grasp. I'd like to say that I stumbled onto that key in a flash, but things seldom happen that way. What really happened was that I began trying to bring my shooting in line with the demands of my body—I would try to be comfortable when I shot. I began concentrating on what felt natural as opposed to what was textbook correct.

This worked better than my greatest expectations. The key was that shooting really was easy; the simplest and most natural techniques worked the best for me. I began winning matches. I didn't necessarily shoot like the other people on the line—I didn't hold the gun in the same way; I didn't stand quite the same way; I didn't have the same shooting style as many of the top competitors. But I won.

It took me four years to go from plinking tin cans to the International Practical Shooters Confederation (IPSC) national championship, which I won in 1980 and again in 1981. What those two championships proved to me was that my style of shooting *works*. It proved that a person with determination, who is willing to work hard, can become a champion.

With my first championship behind me, I began training people, primarily police officers, in my style of shooting. I think of it as a system, able to change when necessary. Modern practical shooting is constantly changing. But even as the courses of fire and the challenges become greater, the basic techniques remain the same. I began teaching my own students, some of whom had been to two or three *other* handgun schools and courses, what I had learned over the past four years. The results were, again, much better than I'd expected. One of my wealthier students, who'd attended several firearms schools across the country, told me he'd learned more in a weekend with me than all his other weeks elsewhere. One police officer credited my training with saving his life in a shooting situation. The response was so overwhelming that I decided to open my own training range, the Mid-South Institute of Self-Defense Shooting, near my home in Memphis. We now offer training in combat handgunning, from the basics to advanced techniques, practical rifle instruction, and combat shotgunning. We're in demand by both civilians and police officers, and the University of Mississippi is in the process of accrediting the MISS facility as a credit course for law enforcement majors.

I feel that if I'd had a book like this when I first started training, my life would have been a lot easier. I'll tell you what works and what doesn't, and I'll teach you the techniques it took me years to develop. I want to tell you up front that no book or school or any amount of instruction can make you a good shot. That's up to you and you alone. But I believe that if you're willing to work and use this book as a starting point, you *can* be a champion. More importantly, if you ever have occasion to draw a firearm in defense of your life, you will have the confidence necessary to *win* that confrontation.

One of the things I like best about IPSC competition is that it is practical. The skills you learn and perfect on an IPSC course can, quite literally, save your life in an armed encounter. That's why my first recommendation is to find out about the IPSC-affiliated club in your area and join up. Once you master the skills in "You Can't Miss," the best thing you can do is begin shooting in a club, in front of people. Nothing will sharpen your skills quite as well.

A second reason for joining the IPSC is that the only way to advance to the Nationals is through accumulating points shooting in club matches. There are five major money shoots each year—the Steel Challenge, the Bianchi Cup, the Second Chance Shoot, the *Soldier of Fortune Magazine* Shoot, and the IPSC National Champsionship. Each one of those matches has its own appeal—- Bianchi is the most money; Second Chance is the most fun to shoot; *Soldier of Fortune* is good for rifle and shotgun assaults; the Steel Challenge is the fastest. Of them all, the IPSC National Championships mean the most to me. Everyone there has proved themselves again and again just for the right to shoot in the Nationals. Just shooting in the Nationals is an honor and something well worth working toward.

Shooting has become more and more of a big league sport in recent years, and I confess to having pushed it in that direction. I was the first shooter to be sponsored by a national magazine *(Soldier of Fortune* backed me in 1981), the first shooter to really urge national manufacturers like Colt to support shooters and the sport, which I think is only fair. No one has benefited more from practical pistol shooting than the manufacturers. Just a couple of years ago a Colt Government Model would sit around on a dealer's shelf for months and months. Now, if you want a .45, you're going to pay a premium price, and that's because of the popularity of combat shooting. Throughout the book I'll be mentioning my sponsors—people who support my shooting and who, in return, I represent—and other reputable people in the gun business who are 100 percent behind IPSC-style shooting. I want to make it clear that I was using and recommending their equipment long before I earned their sponsorship. If they're mentioned in this book, *I have personal knowledge of the people and their products,* and both the people and the products do what they say.

Finally, the greatest thing to me about IPSC-style shooting is that it is still a completely open field. It is the only professional sport where you can quickly become involved and actually have a shot at going all the way to the top. If you want to be a champion bad enough, you can't miss.

About John Shaw

As I was growing up, most of my time was spent with a shotgun in pursuit of quail and dove. Hunting was a way of life growing up in Memphis in the 1960s. It really wasn't until I began college that I rediscovered the handgun, owning my first handgun, a Hawes Single Action .22.

I went to college at the University of Mississippi in Oxford, studying banking and finance. In my spare time, my friends and I studied tin cans, snakes and rabbits, mostly over the iron sights of a High Standard .22 automatic. Every chance we could get we'd head out into the woods around Oxford for a day of plinking, snakes when we could find them, tin cans when we couldn't. That part of Mississippi is home for some of the biggest, fattest cottonmouths in the country, and we did our best to cut their population down.

During the small game season, we hunted rabbits with a handgun and we usually got our share. In fact, as I've said before, I thought I was a pretty good shot—I loved to watch a tin can bounce along the ground while I was shooting it!

I don't know exactly when the pistol bug really bit me, but the closer I got to leaving college, the more involved I became with handguns.

I'd always been athletic, football and baseball and the like, but I was never really committed to those sports. I never really *excelled* in anything. I played sports, but it was never a 100 percent effort, until I found pistol shooting.

I made the decision toward the end of my college years that I was going to become a good pistol shot. Not just good enough to plink rabbits on a Saturday afternoon. I wanted to become a champion.

The first step is believing that you *can* become a champion. The most important step is believing that you have the ability to do something and then translating that belief into an effective program to change belief into reality. Both sides are equally important—it doesn't do you any good to have the best mental attitude in the world if all you do is sit around the house dreaming. Conversely, you can practice until you can barely stand up, but if you're a loser in your mind, all that practice goes to waste.

There are several points that are going to be emphasized over and over again in "You Can't Miss."

The first of these points is to set reasonable goals for yourself. You will need to learn shooting one step at a time. It's not something you can learn in one afternoon. However, it's not something you have to take the rest of your life to learn, either. My

own success is proof of that. Using this book as your guide, take practical shooting one step at a time, getting each one of these techniques down pat before going on to the next.

Another point that I learned early on and can't emphasize enough is to not be afraid of asking questions. When I first began match shooting in local PPC matches, I questioned every good shooter I got close to. I wanted to know what they did and why, because it all had a direct application on what I was teaching myself.

I am completely self-taught, and as I said earlier, I've made most of the mistakes possible.

The problem I found with PPC shooting is that the only people winning were the rangemasters, people who had unlimited ammunition and who actually got paid to spend as much time as possible on the range shooting. No one was paying me for shooting, and I had a family to support.

Before I could get disenchanted with PPC shooting, I discovered practical pistol shooting; I knew I'd found my field. IPSC-style shooting offered more challenges than any other style of shooting I'd encountered. There were moving targets and assault courses, courses shot on metal "reactive" targets and courses shot on paper silhouettes. The shooting required careful planning and strategy as well as a pin-point skill with a gun.

As an added bonus, a good shooter could actually make a little money shooting IPSC matches. The banking and finance major in me liked that a lot.

The more involved I became with combat shooting, the more I realized the sport was just in its infancy. Each year we all learn a little more about what a handgun will do, what a handgun *can* do. It was and still is thrilling.

Combat shooting is one of the very few sports in America open to "outsiders," where a person with determination and the willingness to learn the skills can actually rise to be champion. Shooting with the Tennessee-Mississippi-Arkansas Combat Club, I saw that I could go "all the way."

In 1978 I went heavily into IPSC-style shooting, opening the season with my first big victory, a second-place finish at Bill Wilson's big match in Berryville, Arkansas. I placed just behind Bill and just ahead of then-champion Ray Chapman. I came in fifth at the Second Chance shoot later that year, then sixth at the IPSC Nationals in Los Angeles.

The next year was the first year for the Bianchi Cup, and I

wanted a victory in the worst way. I threw myself into practice for it. I probably shot 10,000 rounds in the month before the match because I wanted it so badly.

As it happened, I blew the match. I'd never been under that kind of pressure before—and I just got the shakes. I'd never missed a Bianchi plate in practice. I missed twelve at the match. I went home from that match a much more humble shooter.

The first Bianchi match taught me the importance of learning to shoot under pressure—the tougher the pressure in practice the better. I learned that a shooter could have all the skills down pat and be impossible to beat on his home court, but if that shooter couldn't overcome the pressure of a big match, he'd never advance to the top ranking.

I also learned something about practice. It's just as easy to practice too much as it is to practice too little. Part of the secret of practicing is learning how to pace yourself, to keep yourself from peaking too soon.

The next year, 1980, was my year. I finished sixth at Bianchi and probably would have finished second if I'd followed some of my own advice and been a little more careful with my ammo. I had pulled every tenth round of my match ammo to check the powder charge and I apparently reassembled one of the rounds without any powder.

On the plates, I was completely clean on the first three distances—you shoot plates at 10, 15, 20, and 25 yards, six plates each. Each distance stage is shot twice and is timed. In the 25-yard stage, I knocked down the first six plates, and when the whistle for the second round blew, I went prone and knocked down the first three plates. I remember thinking, "I've got this made." Then the gun went "putt" instead of "boom," and I saw the bullet lying on the ground about four feet in front of me. By the time I cleared the round, my time had run out. Talk about learning the hard way!

I won the new *Soldier of Fortune Magazine* shoot in 1980, and after that match I learned another important lesson. Mickey Fowler, who was then the IPSC champ, and I decided to try out each others' guns at a nearby range. We shot at 25 yards, offhand, and I thought my three to four inch groups from his Hoag Master was pretty good. He took my Clark Bowling Pin Gun and put six shots *in the same hole.* I knew then that the most important thing about practical shooting was the *basics.* The basics are what I have practiced and taught ever since. I learned that regardless of what some critics might think of IPSC-style shooters, they can hold their own with the best shooters in any other branch of the sport.

The next match was the 1980 IPSC National Championships, and I went into it thinking, "Front sight; squeeze the trigger." I won it, securing not only my first national championship but a spot on the USA team in the next year's world competition in South Africa.

I began 1981 by winning the Steel Challenge, a tough all-metal match sponsored by the Southwest Combat Pistol League. Along with the match came the title of "The Fastest Gun In The World."

I was feeling very confident as I headed into Bianchi. I'd also been practicing—possibly too much—and I made the mistake of letting everybody know how well my practice was going. Everybody was ready to watch me "ace" the 1981 Bianchi Cup matches.

The shakes came again, and my shooting went to pieces. I went home despondent, not even speaking to my wife, Beverly, for about two weeks. "What was I doing," I thought, "devoting all my time to shooting?" Shooting, reloading and practicing had become my life, and my business and my family suffered for it. I realized that what I was doing was wrong, both for me and for my family. I decided that I would retrench and go into the IPSC 1981 National Championships the way I should have gone into every other match, concentrating on the basics and remembering that the only person I was there to beat was myself. If I won, so much the better, but I wanted to walk away from the match knowing that I had done my best, given my all. If I couldn't do that, then I didn't want to shoot anymore.

I went on to win the 1981 IPSC Championship, then finish the year with three gold medals in South African World IPSC competition. I placed second at Second Chance, winning a record eight guns at this one match.

If I never win another championship—a situation I'm doing my best to avoid—I'm proud of my accomplishments in the shooting sports. In addition to my titles and victories, I'm proud of my role in professionalizing practical shooting. When I began shooting, the shooters didn't get any sponsorship from anyone in the business, even though it was the shooting sports business that was benefiting from the publicity around practical shooting. I was the first shooter to be sponsored by a top pistolsmith—Jim Clark and his terrific Bowling Pin Gun—the first shooter to receive match ammunition (from Hornady); the first shooter to suggest to Mike Dillon that his reloading machine should be marketed to individual

World Champions U.S. Gold Team, Johannesburg, South Africa, September, 1981: (from left to right) Mickey Fowler, Ross Seyfried, Mike Plaxco, John Shaw (no beard!) Nick Pruitt. First year U.S. ever won.

shooters; the first shooter to get Colt Firearms involved in the shooting sports—Colt donated specially engraved "One-of-Five" Gold Cups to each member of the USA Gold Team in 1981, of which we are all extremely proud—the first shooter to be totally sponsored by a national magazine, *Soldier of Fortune*, during the 1981 season. In 1982, I'll be sponsored by Gordon Davis, one of my earliest supporters and one of the best holstermakers in the world. With sponsors like shotgun master Garth Choate, Magna-Port-Arms, and the rifle experts at Springfield Armory, I feel like I can't miss!

More important than the personal benefits to me, sponsorship is a good thing for the sport. I think it's great that so many firearms manufacturers, gunsmiths, and accessory people are getting behind practical shooting, and it can't help but benefit us all.

So here's your opportunity to join in. I wish you luck.

Eye/Ear Safety, Zeroing In

Rule One is safety, first and foremost. Practical pistol shooting is in a difficult position. A lot of the more traditional shooters would like to dismiss us as unstable, and the anti-gun media would like to do even more than that. There's also the type of shooting we do—drawing from a holster, rapid fire, speed reloading, changing positions, all providing opportunities for accidental discharges.

Practical shooting as a whole has done an excellent job in keeping its safety record clean, and we all have a responsibility to maintain that record, the best way of changing the minds of some of our critics. Here, then, are the basic rules of safety. Regardless of how many times you've heard them before, it never hurts to hear them one more time:

1) IT'S ALWAYS LOADED! This is especially true for the "bread and butter" gun of practical shooters—the Colt .45 automatic. The .45 is basically a safe gun, probably the safest handgun ever produced. It is not, of course, idiot proof—nothing is. You can't just glance at the gun and tell if it's loaded. *Check every time*—drop the magazine and pull back on the slide slightly to see if there's a round chambered. Some of the newer recoil systems make it nearly impossible to "pinch" the slide and check the chamber. Always check carefully!

2) KEEP THE GUN POINTED DOWNRANGE! Never turn uprange without holstering your gun! At my own range, the Mid-South Institute of Self-Defense Shooting, guns must be holstered unless you're on the firing line under the direction of the rangemaster. The rangemaster is the absolute authority; he does not allow careless mistakes. You will be dismissed from the range for safety violations.

3) WHEN DRAWING FROM LEATHER, MAKE SURE THAT NO PART OF YOUR BODY OR THAT OF A BYSTANDER IS "SWEPT" BY THE GUN BARREL! If that happens in a match, you're disqualified on the spot, which is a lot better than shooting yourself or your best friend. Be especially careful when drawing with the weak hand. (Weak-hand techniques will be covered more extensively later).

4) THINK! Practical pistol shooting is a thinker's as well as a doer's sport. Most gun safety is simply common sense, thinking before you do something stupid.

Another important aspect of safety is eye and ear protection. Always wear glasses to protect your eyes and earmuffs to protect your hearing. Some people, of course, don't have to wear earmuffs—my good friend, gunsmith Jim Clark, who spent many successful years shooting NRA bullseye, doesn't have to wear them, because all those years of shooting left him almost deaf. "We were tough guys back then," Jim says, more than a little ruefully. I thought I was tough, too. I've got the hearing of a 65-year-old man in my left ear from shooting during my college days. Now, *I* wear a set of David Clark silicon-filled hearing protectors—the best I've ever been able to find.

The same goes for glasses. More and more matches are being shot on metal targets, and there is definitely a ricochet factor involved. There's also the danger of a case blowing out or, in some extreme cases, the gun blowing up. After all the tens of thousands of rounds I've spent with a .45, recently my shotgun, a new Browning, blew up on a dove hunt last season. The chamber was apparently oversize, and it let go with a blast and ball of fire right under my nose! One of the other shells went off as well, blowing the receiver to pieces. Accidents happen with even the finest of equipment. My shooting glasses—Bausch and Lomb—saved my eyesight. Browning gave me a new gun and covered my medical expenses. I'm now a complete believer in shooting glasses.

There's been lots of information written on what you need to get started in practical shooting. It's really very simple—you need a good, reliable gun and good practical leather. Gunwise, there's only one way to go, and that's with a Colt Government Model. One advantage of the Government Model is that as you advance in the sport, you can modify the gun to keep up with your progress. Both Jim Clark's super-accurate Bowling Pin Guns and Bill Wilson's Accu-Comp begin life as a stock .45. We'll be going over modifications to the .45 in a separate chapter, but basically you need a gun that'll shoot two-inch groups at 25 yards. When I started out, I didn't even know you *could* shoot two-inches at 25 yards.

Before you do anything to your new gun, shoot it enough—at least several hundred rounds—to know what it will do. It takes a gun that long just to settle in. As for initial modifications, I'd stick to the basics—a good set of fixed sights (Milletts are good) with the appropriate front sight (I prefer a sharply undercut front sight); a good trigger job with a custom long trigger; a throated barrel, and, where necessary, a relieved ejection port. You'll also probably want some sort of speed safety, Swenson or Safari Arms or the like. That will basically get you started and keep you from going broke before you know how you're going to like the sport. As far as sights go, I'd stick to a plain black rear blade and front

RANGE RULES

1. No person(or persons) allowed on Range without Membership Card.
2. No alcoholic beverages or intoxicating drugs allowed on or near Range.
3. No load weapons behind the firing line.
4. NO RIFLES.
5. No Magnum or high velocity loads.
6. No unsafe handling or display of weapons.
7. No vulgar or obscene language.
8. No person under age 21 allowed on the Range unless accompanied by an adult.
9. Ear and Eye protection must be worn at all times.
10. All spectators must remain in designated area.

VIOLATION OF ANY OF THESE RULES WILL CAUSE IMMEDIATE EXPULSION FROM RANGE.

The rules of the range (above) must be followed by everyone to keep the sport safe. Hearing protectors (right) are a must; Clark's are illustrated. Below, a trio of excellent combat handguns, including a Wilson Accu-Comp, a Clark Bowling Pin Gun, and a Gold Cup fitted with Micro sights.

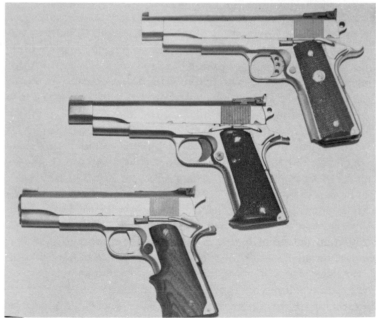

sight. Of course, I know people who swear a loud-colored or dot system front sight has changed their lives—try them, you might like them. But all the top shooters use black.

The same philosophy goes for leather, another topic we'll be covering more extensively in a later chapter. Buy the very best you can afford. I use a cross-draw, but a high-ride hip holster is just as fast. If you have to carry a gun on the street, pick a competition holster that is similar to your duty holster (if you elect not to use your duty holster). Whatever you pick, practice with it until your draw is as smooth and as fluid as it can be—jerky motion is wasted motion.

Your first step is to find out how your gun shoots. One of the things that helped me most when I was starting out was letting an expert shoot my gun. That eliminated my first and favorite excuse—"It's the gun; I'm a great shot"—as well as giving me something to strive toward. I could quickly see what the gun was capable of doing.

You'll quickly see that becoming a good shot requires hours of practice, and large quantities of ammunition. Ammunition is very expensive—reloading your own ammunition is your only solution.

Start at the bottom of the reloading charts and work your way up. What you'll be looking for is one light load for practice and one hardball equivalent load for competition. (See Reloading chapter). There is no need to batter yourself and your gun with a steady diet of hardball. A lot of people don't agree with me on that, but I stand behind it 100 percent.

I'd also suggest slugging your barrel by forcing a soft lead slug through it. There's a surprising amount of variation in .45 auto barrels. Jim Clark tells me he routinely sees as much as .004 variation, and that's enough to make a difference with lead bullets. Lead bullets should be sized .001 over the barrel diameter.

I've never found that hardball shoots that well. Occasionally, you'll come across a gun that loves military hardball, but that is really rare. If you find a lot of hardball that your gun shoots well (assuming you insist on shooting ball), make a note of that lot number and buy as much of the same lot number as you can afford. Each lot tends to shoot differently.

The one exception to the hardball rule is the new Hornady 230-grain flat point bullet. It is one of the most consistently accurate bullets I've ever found—all my guns will shoot it well, which is amazing. In IPSC-sanctioned matches, which require hardball or equivalent, I'd go either with the Hornady flat-point or an equivalent 200-grain lead load (see the Reloading chapter for

Use of good headphones and glasses are most important. Blast kept out by headphones and glasses in case of ricohets.

details). I have learned (the hard way) to avoid 230 round-nose lead bullets; they feed reliably, but their accuracy is terrible.

At the very beginning of your training, try to eliminate as many external variables as possible. If your gun won't shoot well with hardball, feed it something else. If you don't like a cross-draw holster, swap to a high-ride strong hand. Get rid of all the distractions and concentrate on *you*, your skill and your concentration. Never forget that your best competitor is yourself. Take pride in improving yourself.

If you feel like there's a gadget that you just can't live without or that will make you a better shooter overnight, by all means get it and try it. The great thing about competition is that it eliminates the junk. We've all got a collection of things we couldn't live without that ended up as another waste of money. Go ahead and get it out of your system. In fact, drop me a line; I might have one I'll let you have cheap.

Sight Picture

The single most important thing about shooting of any kind is *sight picture*. I say it over and over and over again to my students; I really don't think you can say it too many times. The *sight picture* is where all good shooting begins. What you have to learn to do is focus on your front sight. The rear sight is a blur; the target is a blur. FRONT SIGHT!

Sounds easy, doesn't it? It took me about three years to focus on the front sight, and still, when I miss, it's because I stopped focusing on the front sight. The combination of sight picture and trigger control are the very foundations shooting is founded on. It doesn't matter whether it's IPSC, PPC, or NRA bullseye. The basic principle is unchanged.

The problem is that watching your front sight is not *fun*, especially when you're shooting a moving target or metal plates. Your mind wants your eyes to follow that moving target. Your mind wants to know whether those metal plates fell when you hit them. Sometimes the urge to look at your target is overwhelming. It's so easy to look *over* that front sight and see what's going on out there. Then you miss. In a match, you lose points. In the real world, you lose your life.

One way to test yourself is to go out plinking at tin cans on the ground. If you can see where your bullet hits, you're not watching your front sights. Plinking is loads of fun, but if you're not watching that front sight, then plinking is going to do more harm than good. Everybody wants to raise up to look at what he's shooting at.

There's plenty of time for looking after you've finished shooting. If you must watch, go early and watch all the other competitors' metal plates fall down!

The way I finally taught myself to watch the front sight was by missing a bunch of targets. I kept thinking I had it all down, but the plates just didn't fall. I knew they weren't falling, because I was watching them. When I finally tried not watching them, they started falling.

You've got to watch your front sight. The target needs to be a blur in the background; the front post has to be centered in the rear notch—the same amount of light on either side. I recommend a flat, wide blade on the rear, black with no white line. I've found the white line distracts me. So have other top shooters. I also recommend a sharply undercut front sight, because a ramp sight is bad about reflecting sunlight. I pick up a black front sight as fast as a colored one. The width of the notch and front sight is a very per-

The correct sight picture. Note that only the front sight is in focus.

Two incorrect sight pictures, the first with the target in focus; the second with the rear sight blade in focus.

sonal thing, and after you've been shooting for a while you'll be in a better position to make your own decision. The more I shoot, the less light I like between the front post and the rear blades.

I'd say that 90 percent of the shooting game is the front sight. It's that important.

Whatever it takes to make you look at the front sight is good; do it. Paint it purple, put a little checkerboard on it, stick a white dot up there. Maybe even a picture of a semi-dressed member of the opposite sex—just remember that it's there to make you *watch the front sight!*

To see just how important this is, go to a match or even your local range and just watch the shooters. It's easy to see who's watching the front sight and who's watching the targets. Then compare scores. Bad sight picture is the single biggest and most common mistake any shotter, new or old, makes. Not watching my front sight sank me in the Bianchi Cup in 1981. My concentration slipped, and all of a sudden I was looking at the plates. With six plates in six seconds, things are over pretty quickly. By the time I remembered my front sight, it was too late.

Concentrate! Black everything out in your mind except FRONT SIGHT! (Some shooters tell me that while they're standing on the line, waiting to shoot, they just lower their heads and mumble, "Front sight, front sight," over and over, sort of like a chant.They claim it works.)

This is the most important single lesson you'll learn about shooting.

Trigger Control

Once you're able to see your front sight, you don't want to jerk the sight off the target when you're pulling the trigger. The second basic skill, then, is trigger control. You've got to be smooth on the trigger or you're going to jar off that carefully held sight picture.

You've probably heard "squeeze the trigger" more than any other piece of advice about gunhandling, and it still holds true. For the practical pistol shooter, there are a couple of tough wrinkles. For a start, when you're shooting up close, like the quick two-plate matches at the Steel Challenge, you *can't* squeeze the trigger. There just isn't time. You've got to "slap" it. Then in the next match, when you back up to 50 yards to do some accurate shooting, you slap that trigger and you miss the target altogether.

There's also the problem of the crunch, where you start pulling the trigger with your finger, then just before letoff you crunch the gun with your whole hand, just like you're trying to crush an egg. The bullet will hit the target, but not where it's supposed to hit it.

Imagine your trigger finger is disconnected from the rest of your hand. It moves freely, not affecting or being affected by the other fingers of the hand. Those other fingers are maintaining a constant tension—the same tension all the time—on the gun. The only finger to move is the trigger finger.

I pull the trigger with the outside of the first joint, and that's what I teach my students. Other excellent shooters use the tip of their finger. There are two reasons I use the first joint: First, I've found that using the tip of your finger tends to slow you down in up-close shooting, especially with full-house combat loads. I hate to have two positions for my finger—that just adds too many variables. The second reason is that when I pull with the tip of my finger, it tends to loosen my grip on the gun. I've found that using the first joint gives me a natural feel on the gun, and as a rule, the things that feel the most natural work the best. That is the very heart of my system, and it works!

I use the same trigger pull on both automatics and revolvers, and I recommend endless amounts of dry firing. In fact, dry firing—sighting the gun at a point on the wall or a target and squeezing the trigger—is perhaps the most important exercise you can do to get your shooting in shape. What you are doing, in essence, is "educating" you mind and your finger about how things are supposed to work. If you do enough dry firing, when you get to the range a good trigger squeeze will come naturally. If you can lay your hands on a good air pistol and a metal bullet trap, you can also practice your trigger squeeze (and your sight picture) at home. Since the key to good practical shooting is practice, anything you can do to get that practice time in is going to pay off.

We'll be going into trigger pulls more in our section on modifying the handgun, but there are a couple of general suggestions that apply here. For a match gun, I'd suggest a trigger stop. A trigger stop simply prohibits the trigger from going any further after the sear disengages, and it's an aid to good trigger control. The stop usually takes the form of a set screw in the trigger or in the rear of the trigger guard. For a self-defense gun or, especially, a police gun, I do *not* recommend a trigger stop of any kind. There is the remote possibility that some piece of dirt or material could get between the trigger and the stop, or the screw might loosen, keeping the gun from firing.

Trigger pull is one of those subjects of endless arguments, like which is better, an automatic or a revolver? It's also an area where it is *vitally* important to distinguish between a match gun and a self-defense or street gun. A match gun needs to have the trigger as light as possible, because the lighter the trigger, the less your tendency to slap it. The harder a trigger is, the more you want to jerk it to get it to fire—go out and try to squeeeeezzze an out-of-the-box double action automatic, for example. My first three years I used guns with a trigger pull of between 4.5 and five pounds. Now I'm shooting two or 2.5 pounds. But it takes a very good gunsmith to get a trigger that light in a .45 and make it safe. There's just not that much engagement between the hammer and sear, and no matter *who* does the trigger job, if the slide is dropped without a round in the magazine, the hammer is going to "follow," most of the time, that is, fall from full cock to half cock.

A street gun *must not follow*! You're in that much-dreaded confrontation; you've shot your gun dry and you ram in another magazine, drop the slide and pull the trigger and *nothing* happens! Half-cock! That's why we always have to make the distinction between a purely match gun and a street gun. If your gun does double duty, always err in favor of the street! There are no exceptions to this rule. A self-defense or police gun should *NOT* have a light trigger pull—never less than 3.5 to four pounds. Pulling the trigger had better be a deliberate act, not the function of a muscle twitch. My two regular match guns, a Clark Bowling Pin Gun and a Wilson Accu-Comp, are two of the finest, most accurate .45s made. They'll feed anything and shoot much better than I can. But when I have the occasion to go armed, I *never* carry them, nor do I keep

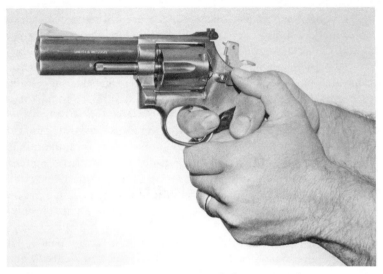

Note the correct position of the trigger finger.

them loaded around the house.

Before I get off triggers, there's just one more point. Once you get a good trigger pull *DO NOT* drop the slide without a loaded magazine in place. Remember I said there wasn't all that much trigger-sear engagement anyway? Dropping the slide is a good way to get even less.

Finally, just a few words on the flinch, anticipating the blast/recoil and actually jerking the gun barrel down. I wish I could offer you a miracle cure—I wish I could offer *me* a miracle cure! There isn't one. Just practice, both live and dry firing. The only way to have a good trigger squeeze is to be *surprised* every time that gun goes off. Suprised! If you anticipate and flinch, you can't win. The old "traditional" solution still works well—load three cylinders of your revolver with live rounds, three with fired rounds, then spin the cylinder. You never know when it's a live round coming up. You can tell quickly if you're flinching, and you can tell when you're cured. The same goes for automatics. Get a couple of magazines and cut the slide stop off, so the slide won't stay back after the final shot (some cheap magazines do this anyway). Load each of them with a different number of rounds. Mix them up and choose one. You won't be able to tell when the last round was fired, which gives the same effect as the revolver practice. Believe me, it will help.

Combat Shooting Stance

The final basic point to master is the combat stance, another area of endless controversy. In fact, it's tough to find two people standing the same way at any given range or match. My own stance goes back to something I mentioned at the very front of the book—shooting is easy. The best stance is the simplest.

In my stance for a right-handed shooter, the left foot is forward and the body is sharply angled, much like a basic boxing or martial arts stance. The important thing here is to be *comfortable*; don't assume a position that puts your body in any sort of strain. For me, that means a sharply angled stance. The right hand comes up and the elbow locks; the left hand supports the right. The left elbow is slightly tucked toward the body.

Get into this position and you'll immediately notice how *stable* your hands are. This is the most stable shooting platform I've ever found. It's the same stance you assume when shooting a rifle or a shotgun, with your strong arm functioning as the stock. In fact, I lay my cheek slightly on my shoulder, same as I would a rifle stock. There's no better position for long-range shooting.

Once you've got the basics of the position mastered, try this: Assume the shooting stance, close your eyes, and without opening your eyes, raise your arms into the proper position. Where are you pointing? Use this procedure to line yourself up on the target. If you're not pointing directly at the target when you open your eyes, shift your feet slightly until you are, so as to avoid any added strain on your muscles. Too many shooters twist this way and that way to line their gun up, and after a few shots you can see them straining to hold the position they're in. Remember that shooting is easy, and you want to find the easiest position to get into, plus the most comfortable position to be in once you're there.

The advantage to such a stable shooting platform is that you never have to move your feet when shooting at a multiple or moving target: Just pivot your body at the hips. The platform remains steady.

The only variation on this stance that I ever use is when shooting very quickly. In that case, my strong-hand elbow may not be locked for the first shot. I lock it in place, though, as soon as I can.

Another thing you want to remember is to raise the gun up to your head. Make the gun come up; don't keep putting your head lower and lower. The gun should be up at eye-level, and your cheek should be resting on your shoulder. It's a very natural position, and you'll be amazed how quickly you can get into it.

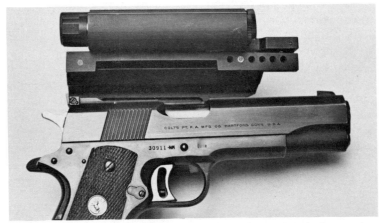

The most advance sighting system in the manual. I use aim-points on revolvers and auto's. Second overall at 1982 Bianchi Cup was taken with one of these and I predict 1983 cup will be won with one.

You also want to remember to lean *slightly* into the recoil. The reason is that it puts you more in control, using your body's weight to damp the gun's recoil. If you're pushing forward, you'll be able to come on with the second shot much, much quicker. Don't lean too far forward or you'll unbalance the platform—it'll be harder to pivot from the hip.

Another thing to avoid is the crouch. You see this stance used on television, but think about what is happening when you crouch. You've introduced a whole new series of movements into the shooting equation: The body going down, the gun coming up. The more complicated a maneuver is, the less likely you are to do it successfully under the pressure of a match or a life-threatening situation.

It's important here to take a page from the martial artists; simplicity is very, very important. You want to use the fewest possible motions to get to where you want to go. Avoid crouching or twisting your feet into strange positions. Don't raise the gun *above* your line of sight—a holdover from bullseye shooting, where it helps with breath control—then back down onto the target. That's just adding an additional, and unnecessary, movement. Don't do anything that feels unnatural to you, because more than likely your body is right.

Never forget that shooting is easy.

Grip and Fire Control

The combat shooter doesn't have a lot of time to fumble with gripping the gun. When drawing a holstered weapon, it's important to hit it right the first time. You don't have the luxury of picking the gun up and putting it down until it feels just *right*. Appropriately, the best grip is the quickest and most natural feeling.

The best way I've found to achieve this grip is to just grab the gun hard while it's still in the holster. It's like making a fist with the gun in the middle. As the gun comes out and the strong-hand thumb knocks off the safety, the weak hand comes over to grab the strong hand around the gun. the weak-hand thumb pushes *down* on top of the strong-hand thumb, and the weak-hand index finger pushes *up* on the bottom of the trigger guard. This gives you a very strong, very stable grip.

It's a grip that also does an excellent job of controlling heavy recoil. A lot of combat shooters extend their weak-hand index finger to wrap around the front of the trigger guard; in fact, many guns now have a hook-shaped trigger guard or checkering on the front of the guard just for that purpose. I've found, though, that it's much *harder* to control a gun in heavy recoil with the weak-hand index finger stuck out there. What usually happens is the recoil dislodges the finger and the whole grip is shaken, sometimes even broken. I do know some shooters who do an excellent job of shooting with the finger around the trigger guard, but they also shoot several thousand rounds a year.

One of the other advantages of my system is that no part of the weak hand is either stuck out and exposed or in contact with any of the moving parts of the gun. The thumb is really the weakest part of the body—ask any police officer who's had the occasion to lead somebody around by the thumb. Any grip that exposes one of the thumbs is potentially dangerous; better both thumbs should be safely tucked away.

My grip also works for either revolvers or automatics, which is a definite plus if you enjoy shooting a lot of different kinds of guns, as I do. Again, the key word is simplicity. My grip is stable and safe, plus the added bonus of not requiring any particular modification to the gun for it to work. Grab the gun with one hand, then grab it with the other. What could be simpler?

You want to grip the gun as tightly as you can without trembling. I used to squeeze a rubber ball all the time, and it helps in building up the strength required for shooting. I've recently begun working out with weights to increase the strength in my arms and hands. The advantage to weights is that they make even the heaviest

Use this grip for either revolvers or automatics—note the correct placement of hands and fingers.

match gun seem light by comparison.

I think if more people adopted this grip style, the number of competitive shooters in the sport would increase. For the casual shooter, the grip works well with everything from .22s to .44 mags.

Another advantage is the grip works for any gun. I want to be able to shoot well with *anything* I pick up, not just a "trick" match gun. In fact, I prefer a revolver to an automatic, just because I like the way a revolver feels in my hand. As a combat shooter, your goal should be to hit the x-ring with whatever is placed in your hand, be it a Clark Bowling Pin Gun or an out-of-the-box Chief's Special.

Smooth, Quick Draw

If you really work at it, you'd be amazed at how complicated you can make the simple act of drawing a pistol from a holster. Part of the problem, of course, is television. Ever since there has been television, good guys and bad guys have been making a production out of whipping a shootin' iron out of leather. The secret of a good, smooth combat draw, though, is *not* to make a big production out of it. No flourishes, no flailing of arms, no wasted moves.

The secret of a good combat draw is to minimize all your motions. The fewer motions you have, and the shorter those motions are, the quicker your draw will be. If you first concentrate on smoothness, speed will follow. DO NOT TRY TO BE A QUICK-DRAW ARTIST! Leave that for the real quick-draw artists who have metal bullet deflectors built into their holsters.

The number one factor to consider in any draw is *safety*. If the gun barrel sweeps any part of your own body or that of a bystander, it is not a safe draw, and YOU ARE DOING SOMETHING WRONG! No exceptions here, ever.

I begin my draw with both hands slightly raised. It's a natural-feeling position and easy to move from. At the signal, the strong hand—in my case, the right—moves toward the holstered gun. I keep that movement as simple as possible. In fact, I try not to move my strong side upper arm at all; rather, my lower arm pivots on the elbow.

The weak hand, meanwhile, stays in a raised position, helping to counterbalance the movement of my strong hand. A lot of shooters grab the cross-draw holster with their weak hand, but this is wrong. It places your weak hand in danger of being swept by the gun barrel, and it adds an unnecessary movement to the draw.

Another point here: If I know where my targets are, such as in a match, I usually look *down* at the gun while I'm waiting for the signal to draw. That way, my hand knows exactly where it's going when it starts to move. In addition, it keeps my eyes focused on something close at hand, which makes it much easier to pick up the front sight. If you're focused on the target, your eyes have to refocus to get on the all-important front sight. I know I'll be on-target when the gun comes up because I will have already checked my stance and aligned myself correctly. If I have to be watching my target, I'll always glance down before I draw to orient my hand.

As the strong hand comes up with the gun—ideally all part of the *same* motion; I want to think in terms of one movement rather than start, stop, start—my strong-hand thumb knocks off the safe-

On pages 37, 38 and 39 we show the proper sequence for drawing crossdraw and drawing from the hip. The crossdraw sequence, explained in the text, begins on page 38, then goes to page 39, with the final two photos on page 38. The photo at right is a perfect example of what NOT to do. Keep the weak hand clear at all times.

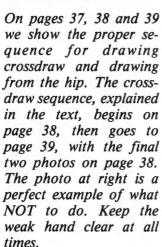

ty about six to eight inches *OUT* of the holster. NEVER THUMB THE SAFETY OFF A .45 WHEN THE GUN IS IN THE HOLSTER! By my own tests, you don't gain a thing on speed and you increase the risk of an accidental discharge.

My weak hand then grabs the strong hand and I *push* my arms forward, locking my strong-side elbow. I'm ready to go.

The procedure is exactly the same for drawing from a hip holster, with the exception that the strong-side elbow moves backward to allow the draw. Think of it as a circular motion: The strong-side hand drops down, grabs the gun, and pulls the gun forward and up. Again, the safety stays on until the gun is well clear of the holster.

The draw is where a good holster really pays off. The best holsters are anchored so solidly that they stay in place, yet they release the gun smoothly during your draw.

Remember what I said about not trying to be a quick-draw artist. One of my favorite pastimes is watching other shooters shoot, and I've spent a lot of time analyzing the way I myself shoot. My speed comes from my ability to quickly pick up the front sight and get off that first shot: I would not class my own draw as blindingly fast but I am consistently quick on the first shot. I believe, then, that while the draw is very important, the basics are even more so. The ability to quickly pick up the front sight and tighten up on the trigger will more than make up for a less-than-superfast draw.

Concentrate on smoothness and conservation of motion in all your practice. Don't push yourself for speed until your body is "educated" to the movements of the draw. It goes back to the practice of martial arts, where the basic movements are constantly practiced until they become automatic. Practice until the draw becomes a single motion, a smooth reflex. You'll be surprised at how fast you actually are.

Speed Reloading

In a lot of ways speed reloading resembles the speed draw. The goal in each is to minimize movement, and keep whatever movement that is necessary as smooth as possible. Whether with an automatic or a revolver, you want to reduce the act of reloading into the fewest simple motions, then practice those motions until they become automatic.

Reloading a Colt-type automatic is easy: After you've fired the last shot and the slide locks back, the weak hand goes to the belt and pulls free the fully charged magazine. The strong-hand wrist, meanwhile, turns about five degrees *clockwise* and slightly back toward the body, allowing the thumb to punch the magazine release. (Most match guns will have an extended or enlarged magazine release button to make this operation easier. I do *not* recommend an extended release button on a street gun because of the danger of the button being tripped by the holster.) The strong-arm elbow may bend slightly, but do not lower the gun from eye level.

In a typical magazine pouch, the magazine is bottom up. All magazines have base pads. The weak hand grabs the bottom of the magazine with the index finger and the thumb pointed downward to the top of the magazine. As the new magazine comes up, the base of the magazine is seated firmly against the palm of the weak hand. Using the thumb and index finger as a guide, the magazine is shoved into the well and seated with a hard slap by the palm. I usually hit the *rear* of the magazine well first—it's a simpler motion than hitting the front and having to cock the weak-hand wrist, which risks stripping a round out of the new magazine.

You'll notice that the weak hand automatically assumes the proper grip after inserting a magazine this way. The gun has never fallen below eye-level, so you're quicker coming back onto the target. This should take less than one second, shot to shot.

With a revolver, you'll be reloading with your strong hand instead of the weak. After the last shot is fired, open up the revolver, point the barrel straight up, and, using the thumb of the weak hand, punch the empties out. The strong hand, in the meantime, goes for the speedloader. As the hand comes up with the speedloader, the weak hand flips the gun over—the barrel is now pointing straight down and the speed loader is inserted. The gun is brought back into battery. This is going to take a couple of seconds.

The best thing to do here is study the pictures we've included and practice *slowly*. As with the draw, once you've got the motions down, the speed will follow. There's obviously a much greater

(Preceding page) The rapid reload for a revolver—note the barrel of the gun pointing first vertically, then horizontally. The way to quickly reload an automatic (above). Note the position of the strong-hand elbow and the weak-hand fingers. The spent magazine is shown falling in the second photo.

---

chance of fouling up the revolver reload, and I would suggest that you police officers who must use a revolver practice this method extensively. It might take a fraction longer to be sure that the gun is first pointed straight up, then straight down, but it is important. In dumping the empties, it's better to let gravity help as much as possible. It greatly increases the likelihood that all the rounds are going to be knocked clear. Same thing for letting gravity help with the reloading itself. If the gun is pointed straight down, those rounds are going into the chambers where they belong.

Clearing Jams

No way around it, jams are going to happen. Even if your gun is 100 percent and you're using factory ammo, there's always a chance that *something* will go wrong—remember Murphy's Law. A recent shooting session with Jim Clark, the gunsmith, and his son, Jim, a fine shot in his own right, is a good example. We were using Clark Bowling Pin Guns and were having smokestack trouble because my pratice loads were too light for the heavy recoil spring in his gun. We did have a lot of *primo* factory match ammunition, so we shifted to that. We quickly experienced not one, but two failures to fire—no powder in the factory loads. At one of 1981's matches, a top shot lost a lot of money because a factory round failed to fire. The primer went off, but the bullet didn't go anywhere. Turned out there was no flash hole. Proving that if you shoot as much ammunition as you should, sometimes things fail. You need to know what to do.

The most common jam is the smokestack, the empty hull lodged straight-up in the ejection port (hence the same). The usual cause of a smokestack jam is underpowered ammunition or a recoil spring that's too stiff. The way to clear it is to reach up with the weak hand and strip the case off the gun, pulling the slide back as well. As the case flies loose, the slide rams forward and chambers another round—most of the time. If you're shooting off a barricade, scrape the case off against a barricade. If necessary, *scrape the case off against your leg.*

The two other kinds of jams are a bit more serious—failure to feed and failure to extract. A failure to feed is the easiest jam to *prevent*. If you're going to be in a match, run every single round you plan to use through the gun, being *extremely* careful not to blow a hole in your floor. All safety precautions apply *doubly* here. You'll know in advance that every round will feed. In keeping a gun for defense, the same idea applies. Don't just stick a new batch of ammunition in your defense gun and put it away. Try the ammunition first—this applies to both revolvers and automatics. It's a simple rule, and one that's violated too many times.

If you do get a feed jam, first see if the round can be forced into place with your hand striking the back of the slide. If it can't, drop the magazine, lock the slide back, shake the round out of the mag well, letting it fall, insert a new magazine, and release the slide. Yes, as a matter of fact, it is slow, which is why you want to prevent this sort of thing from happening.

Another type of failure to feed is the case that is slightly ballooned or oversized for the chamber, such as on the IPSC California.

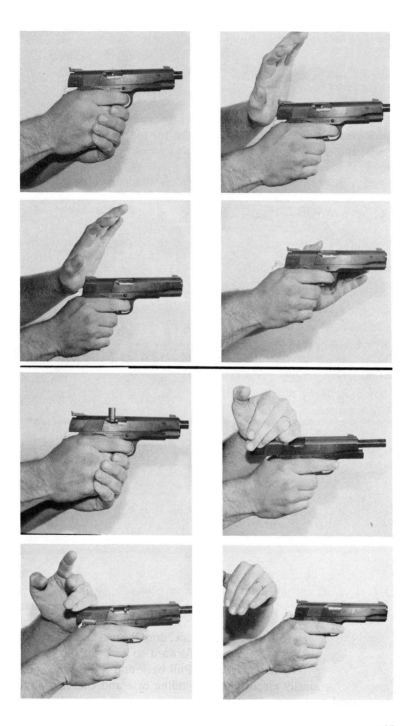

(Preceding page, top) A failure-to-close jam, using the butt of the hand to close the slide; (preceding page, bottom) the most common jam, a smokestack, using the weak hand to strip off the round and cycle the slide. Above, a failure to feed, the most disastrous type of jam. See text for full clearing sequence.

circuit where hot loads are the norm. Those super-throated match guns and hot loads create .45 caliber "belted magnums." If the case enters the chamber of your gun but won't seat, rap the rear of the slide and try to force it home. If that doesn't work, pull back the slide and eject the round. If you've got a long ejector, as do most match guns, the procedure is a bit more complicated. You're going to have to drop the magazine and get the round out the bottom. But be careful—if the round slips off the extractor, the live primer can be forced against the sharp end of the ejector. IT CAN AND HAS FIRED! When you're trying to eject a live round, don't just slam the gun around and try to jar it loose!

A failure to extract, which is not all that common, is the worst jam you can get. You've got a case in the chamber and a live round coming up behind it. Lock the slide back, drop the magazine to get rid of the live round. Slam the slide forward to pick up the lodged case, then insert a new magazine. Pull back and release the slide once more, ideally ejecting the offending case and chambering a live round.

46

Multiple Targets

Multiple targets do much to build your practical shooting skills. The ability to hit several targets at varying ranges is also an important aspect in building your confidence not only in matches but for self-defense situations as well.

There's no magic in shooting multiple targets—all the basics apply equally to single targets, multiple targets and moving targets. Again, concentrate on your front sight. That's harder to do with multiple targets than with a single target because your mind wants to watch the proceedings, especially with reactive metal targets.

Metal targets are the wave of the future in practical shooting, although strict IPSC courses are shot with regulation cardboard silhouettes. Pioneered by John Bianchi for his Bianchi Cup match, metal plates have won widespread acceptance because they are fun to watch. Rather than waiting until the end of the match for scoring, the audience can see immediately how a particular shooter is doing. Secondly, reactive targets are fun for the shooter—when they're hit, they go down, summoning up images of the old carnival shooting gallery.

So you've got to be prepared for two kinds of multiple targets—the paper targets and the metal reactive targets. You want to concentrate on the same two things for both: Front sight and a quick shot. In going from target to target, you want your movement to be smooth and concise. Pivot the top half of your body without changing your grip or your stance—that's the advantage of the grip and stance we taught in the "Basics" chapters. Shoot as soon as your front sight comes on target, but be careful to concentrate on each shot. One of the dangers in multiple targets is to mistime your shot on a middle target because you're already thinking about the next target on down the line. An edge shot on a metal plate will usually knock it down, but an edge shot on the larger "Pepper Poppers" will not.

You don't have time usually to wait and see if the target falls. If you leave a target standing, come back to it after the last target is shot. You're less likely to break your concentration doing that than by checking each shot.

When allowed, always go from left to right, because that's the way the gun is recoiling. I was one of the first shooters to do just that, and it helped my speed tremendously. You're not fighting the gun nearly as hard, and you can be back on target much quicker.

In a match like the Steel Challenge, where there are several metal targets at varying distances, I usually shoot the closest target *first*. When you shoot the easiest target first, it helps settle you

down and establish your rhythm. You might be a little rattled from the draw or from match pressure, and if you go for the hardest target first and you miss it, it can ruin your whole set. If you go for the easiest first, it helps build your confidence—"Well, I got *that* one!"

In a match like the Steel Challenge, shooting the easiest target first takes preference over my "left to right" rule. I think it's more important to get rid of the match shakes.

Finally, resist the temptation to "force" the last shot. If you force the shot by breaking your rhythm and trying to rush it, more likely than not you'll miss. Forcing the final shot is one of the main mistakes shooters make on multiple targets. In trying to pick up an extra half-second, they cost themselves the whole match. A smooth rhythm is what you're going for here—don't forget it.

Remember to always line up on the *middle* of the course—you don't want to put your body in a strained position by the time you get to the last shot. Strive for accurate placing of each shot, and don't look back. If you've mastered the basics, your shots will be there when it comes time to total up the score.

Moving Targets

The basic technique with a moving target is identical to the technique with a stationary target—concentrate on keeping your target a blur and your front sight on the same spot on the target. The reason a moving target seems harder to some shooters is that the eye wants to follow a moving target much worse than a still target. It is harder to concentrate on your front sight when your eye is being drawn to something moving in the background. Once you're able to concentrate on that front sight, however, you will find that the moving target is a snap.

One of the first things you want to do is line your stance up in such a way that you're pointed at roughly the mid-point of the target's run. If you're lined up for the beginning of the target's run, you'll have to break your stance to continue shooting as the target heads for the end of its run. If you're aligned toward the middle, however, you can twist from the waist in either direction, and you don't have to worry about putting a strain on your shooting stance and grip.

Obviously, you're going to have to *lead* a moving target. Lead simply means that because of the motion of the target, you're going to have to shot in front of where you want the bullets to go. With a target moving at 10 feet per second, which is a standard speed for many moving targets, you'll have to aim *one foot* in front of where you'd like your bullets to impact if you're using .45 hardball from 25 yards. That's probably far more than you thought you'd need. From 10 yards, you'd have to lead four or five inches; from 15 yards, seven or eight inches.

Lead is a function of velocity, obviously. The faster a bullet is going, the sooner it's going to get to the target. A 200-grain hardball equivalent load, which is moving at a higher velocity than 230-grain hardball, only requires about nine inches of lead.

A standard velocity .38 Special, the police issue ammunition, also requires almost a full foot's lead at 25 yards, which is one of the reasons even some good police officers who are watching their front sights miss.

The best way to learn how to shoot a moving target is to set one up and practice. While that sounds a little scary at first, we've included in our chapter on "Practice" plans for an excellent moving target for under $300! The target is so good that several police departments in my area have adopted it, some after having much trouble with their multi-thousand dollar movers that stayed broken down. Our moving target is the essence of simplicity — a reversible electric motor, nylon rope, and a steel cable. There's

The moving target carrier.

nothing to get shot to pieces except replaceable wood slats, the speed can be varied through the use of different pulleys on the motor, and the whole thing can be put together in a single afternoon. There's really no excuse for *not* having one.

Learning to shoot moving targets is one of the most useful skills you'll learn from practical pistol shooting, especially if you're involved in handgun hunting. A moving deer in a dense wood is one of the toughest shots a handgunner can make, but steady practice on the range with the mover can make all the difference in the world. You'll be shocked to see just how much lead you have to give a deer who's really in a hurry (about two feet at 25 yards with a moderate load).

When the target comes out from the right-side barricade, you want to immediately begin tracking the target with your gun. Most shooters, myself included, don't open fire on the target until it's nearing the midpoint of its run, then we quickly shoot the specific number of shots. With practice, shooting a moving target is very similar to rapid-fire shooting of a stationary target.

The two main points are 1) force yourself to concentrate on that front sight regardless of the distraction a moving target offers, and 2) strive for a smooth, steady tracking motion with your gun, remembering to turn your body *from the waist*. Do not alter your stance during the firing sequence.

50

Weak Hand/Strong Hand

Shooting with the weak hand and the unsupported strong hand are integral parts of practical pistol shooting. Most weak-hand/strong-hand matches take place at 15 yards or less, so a perfect sight picture or perfect trigger control isn't necessary.

Part of how you approach weak-hand/strong-hand shooting depends on the type of match. There are some switch-hand matches, three shots weak hand, three shots strong hand, and I'd like to deal with them first. The reason is that such matches require a "compromise" stance, facing the target square on. That stance allows you to get a reasonable sight picture with both hands. When swapping hands, I keep my other arm extended for balance.

In a weak-hand-only match, you'll first have to draw with your weak hand. Study the photographs carefully. Here is where a cross draw holster really pays off. As you go for your gun, you twist the lower portion of your arms a full 180 degrees, grab the gun properly, and pull it forward to draw. As your weak arm comes up with the gun, rotate the gun into the proper position, being careful not to sweep any part of your body or a bystander with the barrel of the gun. With a crossdraw, that's pretty easy to do. With a high-ride hip holster, it's much, much harder. You have to reach all the way across your body to draw the gun, making sure that the strong hand arm is safely out of the way. I flatly recommend a crossdraw holster for any weak-hand matches.

When shooting with the weak hand, stay in the basic, natural stance. Grip the gun exactly the same way you do with the strong hand—tight, but not tight enough to cause the muscles of the arm to quiver. You'll have to cock your head toward the weak side to get a good sight picture, and it's a good idea to lean slightly more forward than you would in a two-hand hold. Keep your strong hand in a position to help you counterbalance—usually slightly forward and bent at the elbow, as if the hand were getting ready to go forward to assume a two-hand grip.

Try for a trigger squeeze, but you probably won't make it. I try to make my weak-hand trigger squeeze as smooth as I can, but it's nowhere near as precise as my strong hand.

When shooting strong-hand only, I take a tip from the old NRA bullseye shooters and turn my strong side toward the target with my feet in an almost 90-degree position, the strong side foot pointed toward the target. I lean forward into the gun when I shoot and keep my weak hand bent at the elbow and slightly raised for balance.

The proper sequence for the weak-hand draw as described in the text.

Prone Shooting

Prone shooting is a technique of which far too many handgunners never take advantage. On the practical side, it's the most stable position for long-range shooting for the handgun hunter, and it offers the smallest amount of body exposure in a self-defense situation where no cover is available.

At the 1981 World Shoot in South Africa, we found that the South African shooters would drop into the prone position whenever possible, much more, in fact, than any of the American shooters. The reason American shooters avoid the prone position is that they think it takes too long to assume the position. In actuality, with practice you should be able to drop into a prone position in approximately one second, getting your first shot off in less than 2.5 seconds.

When you go prone, drop to the weak-side arm and strong-side knee, then push your feet out from under you. Complete your grip, aim, and shoot.

Try to keep your shoulders parallel to the line of fire. Push your feet to the left and tuck your right leg slightly up underneath your body.

One of the mistakes most shooters make in the prone position is they place both their elbows on the ground, but their hands gripping the gun are up in the air, which is a wobbly situation at best. To counteract this, I change my grip slightly, rolling my weak hand almost directly underneath the gun. I then place my weak hand on the ground, which is almost as stable as shooting from a benchrest. I then rest my cheek on my strong arm, sight, and fire.

When dropping into a prone position, avoid placing your weak hand squarely on a rock, or in a low spot as I did in the 1981 *Soldier of Fortune* match. It was on a close sequence with not too much time—so little time, in fact, that there was nothing I could do but shoot. It didn't work.

Otherwise, the prone position is the way to go if there's time or if there's a long shot involved.

Notice weak-hand slides under gun so it can rest on ground, index finger is no longer under trigger guard.

53

The prone position.

Barricade Shooting

Shooting a .45 automatic off a barricade is one of the hardest aspects of practical pistol shooting to do well. The temptation is to place some portion of the gun against the side of the barricade itself. If you give in to that temptation, the best you can hope for is a clean miss, plus being completely unable to come back on the target quickly.

The best advice for barricades, if the target is close, in the ten-yard range, is don't touch the barricade at all. It is faster to sight and shoot at a close-in target with either your strong hand or your weak hand if you don't touch the barricade. You will obviously be in a strained position, but that will be offset by the closeness of the target. Keep your hand far enough from the barricade so recoil doesn't slam your hand into the barricade.

For a longer shot from a barricade, you're going to need a more stable position for shooting. The most stable position I've ever found for barricade shooting (strong side) is to press the back of the weak hand strongly into the side of the barricade. Again, you're in a strained position, but if you use enough pressure the gun will remain absolutely steady.

I alter my grip for weak-hand shooting off a barricade. I grip the gun with my strong hand, but instead of wrapping my weak hand around the grip, I grab my strong-hand wrist with my weak hand and hold tightly. This provides a reasonably stable platform for getting the weak-hand shot off, and again, most weak-hand shooting will be at close ranges.

You'll also have to deal with a Rhodesian wall, which is a wall eight feet by eight feet with an 18-inch window cut 56 inches high. There's a four-foot-wide, one-foot-high step just below the window, and a thick, knotted rope hanging from the top-center of the wall. You shoot strong side, weak side, and through the window. The strategy for strong side and weak side is the same: Hold onto the rope with the opposite hand, lean to the proper side, and shoot either strong hand or weak hand, depending on the side called for. Use the rope to pull yourself *into* the wall, which helps to stabilize your shooting position. This is one type of shooting that's easier than it looks.

The strategy for shooting through the window applies to shooting through *any* window. For close-up shots, the same rule applies as with the barricades—don't use the window at all. Assume the proper grip and stance, shoving the gun through the window but not touching any part of the window. You want the gun to go as far as possible through the window to protect you

Strong-side (above) and weak-side barricade shooting. Remember not to rest the gun against the barricade.

from the muzzle blast and to protect the gun from recoiling into the top of the window, which could damage the sights. For a long shot through the window, also follow the same procedure as barricades, which is placing the weak hand firmly against the left (in my case) side of the window. Do *not* rest the gun on the bottom of the window sill. Although it is the most obvious position for the gun, it works the worst. The problem is that it is hard to get the gun back into position for a second shot, and it is no more stable than a braced position against the weak side.

Instinct and Hip Shooting

In reality, advanced techniques are really more of the same, only faster and more furious. After mastering both the basics of shooting and the basic combat techniques, the dedicated shooter will want to concentrate on *speed* and *movement*. You want to shoot faster, and you want to be able to move quickly from position to position. Both these things require a solid grasp of all the techniques we've discussed earlier—if you have to think about the basic techniques, it is almost impossible to apply them while you're running from point to point or racing through an assault course. Practice the three basics and the nine combat techniques until they are second nature! Then you're ready for speed and movement.

One of the advanced techniques you'll need to be familiar with is also one of the most "mysterious," and that is hip shooting. In my opinion, hip shooting has very limited utility. There are a number of shooters in this country who can do amazing things with a gun from the hip, but they are few and far between. In practical shooting, you are usually scored on a Comstock count, which takes into account both speed and score. Being fast isn't enough. In a real shooting situation, a misplaced shot could cost you your life. I cannot say it too many times: Aimed fire is almost as fast and much more accurate than shooting from the hip.

Where is hip shooting useful? When ranges are less than three yards, such as when you're charging a target on an assault course, hip shooting is the answer. I call it "shove" shooting, though, because you want to "shove" the gun straight at the target, firing when your arms are fully extended. If the target is beyond three yards, aim and fire.

The other use for a hip shot is in a metal plate match where two plates are close together vertically and you must shoot both in the quickest possible time. Shove the gun forward at the bottom plate and fire, then assume the proper stance and fire at the upper plate. Actually, it takes place so fast that the draw and both shots should be one single motion, with the recoil from the first shot pulling your hand into position for the second shot.

In a shooting confrontation in the real world, remember that three-yard limit. In a narrow hallway or a close quarters situation, hip shooting is an alternative—but a last ditch alternative. If you must use it, don't go into a crouch or make any unnecessary movements at all—just shove and shoot.

I have to confess that despite all the shooting I've done with a .45, I can't consistently hip-shoot metal plates from seven yards. Regardless of what you've read or been told before, don't bet your life on a hip shot.

The proper way to hip shoot. Remember the three-yard limit.

Night Shooting

More and more ranges that have the facilities are offering night shoots, and I can't think of any type of match that will help you more in real-life shooting situations. For the homeowner, most confrontations with intruders take place during the nighttime hours in either no-light or dim light situations. That also holds true for police officers, who too many times find themselves going into dangerous dark situations with sights they can't see.

Most night courses are shot at fairly close ranges, 15 yards and in, and, obviously, you're not expected to shoot the course in as fast a time as during the day. A typical night course might require you to hit three targets with one shot each at five yards, which should take about 2.5 seconds; two shots each on three targets at ten yards, which should take about five seconds—in other words, taking two to four seconds longer for you to find your sights.

The only way to go in night is with the radium Nite-Site, a self-luminous green sight element that glows in the dark. The darker it gets, the better it glows. On adjustable sights, a luminous bar or dot is inserted just below the rear sight notch, and a luminous green dot is placed in the front sight. In low light, center the dot on the bar, place the front sight dot on the target, and fire.

In addition to being simple to use, Nite-Sites are also simple and inexpensive to install. I not only have them on my competition guns, but on my defense shotguns and an AR-15 as well. I can't imagine a police officer *not* having one.

Some of our matches are being shot in *dim-light* situations, and that's where luminescent paint comes into its own. There are various kinds and colors of paint that glow in low-light. The best, if you can find it, is watchmakers' paint used to paint the hands of watches.

One general point to remember is to allow your eyes to become used to the dark before entering the dark room where the match is being held. I use dense sunglasses before a match to ease the transition from light to dark.

If you've trained yourself to watch that front sight, you'll be able to see the front sight and its relation to the target during the muzzle flashes. One of the advantages of a Nite-Site is that you don't lose the green dot even during muzzle flash.

Assault Courses

Assault courses are where you have to put everything together. All the techniques, all the equipment involved in practical pistol shooting get their toughest wringing out in assault courses. Everything has to work and work together, and when it does, you can see the results of all your training.

I find assault courses the most challenging and the most fun part of practical shooting, and I think I'm the top assault course person in the country. It's easy to make a mistake on an assault course, because there are so many elements to coordinate at the same time. How fast should you run? Is the target close enough to hip-shoot or should you aim and fire? What's the best way to climb over or approach a barricade? Should you reload on the run or wait until you stop? Do you want to risk heading into the final target with only a few shots in your gun?

The best way to beat these and all the other problems associated with assault courses is to plot the whole thing out five or six times in advance of your going to the line. I know that's advice I've given before, but it is *super* important for assault courses. You have to plan every single shot, every single step along the way. I go step by step. I see my front sight on every target, pull the trigger in my mind every time.

If I don't, I'm asking for a disaster. In the 1981 season I finished second in an assault course at the IPSC nationals just because I didn't think it out enough. There was a Rhodesian wall that had to be climbed, and I'd never climbed a wall like that before. I had everything else planned out, but for some reason I decided that I would worry about that wall when I got to it. I even planned everything after the wall, so I wasn't worried. Everything ran like clockwork, and I got to the wall and in one step was on top of it. I couldn't believe how easy it was! The problem was the three targets you had to shoot from the top of the wall. I'd never shot those targets in my mind, and it was a jolt. I had to *think* about them, and I shot at one 35-yard target five times before I hit it. My failure to think out those three targets cost me the match. I was lucky that I had such a large lead in the nationals that it didn't cost me the championship.

My first and most important recommendation, then, on assault courses is to take some time before the match to think the course out. Imagine yourself running each phase and plan what you're going to do at each one. Plan where to reload and where you'll have to holster your gun. Plan which foot you want to hit a wall with, and be sure to start on the correct foot so you'll end up

the way you want. DO NOT OVERLOOK ANY DETAIL, NO MATTER HOW SMALL. Not if you want to win.

My second recommendation is to be sure of all your equipment, from your hat to your gun. Make sure your ear and eye protection will stay on when subjected to the stresses of running and jumping. You'd be surprised at how many competitors lose valuable seconds because their earmuffs start falling off their heads or their shooting glasses slide down on their noses.

Again, I recommend loose clothes and a good pair of sneakers or running shoes. It's best to get shoes designed for competitive sports played on a grass field rather than in a gym, as the tread pattern will be better suited to running and jumping.

The assault course will give your leather a major workout. The gun and magazines must stay put. There's nothing more embarrassing or frustrating than reaching down for a magazine that's not there. If the gun's not there, you're disqualified. It's here in assault courses that having the best pays off.

You should always carry more ammunition than you need. If the course requires five magazines, I always carry seven. When you are moving as quickly as you'll have to be, it's easy to drop a magazine. If you have to stop and pick that magazine up in order to finish the match, you're going to lose many precious seconds. Better to be able to reach down and grab a spare. As I said, always carry two magazines more than the course requires. It's a good habit to get into.

A lot of shooters think that to win assault courses, you've got to be a sprinter. I think just the opposite. The last thing you want to do is run flat out, thinking you're going to pick up time. What happens is that when you arrive at the firing point, it's harder to stop and get set to shoot. Your motions are jerky and, in some cases, you'll be out of breath. In short, you'll lose all the time you picked up by sprinting flat out.

What I recommend is a controlled run. I try to take long, loping steps aimed at not tiring myself out and being ready to shoot as soon as I arrive on station. I want to be able to shoot the second I stop moving, and the only way to do that is to keep *from* sprinting.

I start slowing down about ten yards before I get to the firing point to make sure I'm going to arrive in the right position. When I hit the firing point, I want to be in the correct stance that we outlined earlier. Shifting your position once you've arrived at the firing point costs time. You also want to keep your motions smooth and natural. Smooth motions take less time than jerky motions.

Long smooth steps get you there just as fast and a lot more controlled to shoot.

Don't use the barricades for close targets. It takes as much as one second more to set up on the barricade than to just lean around and shoot. Reread the chapter on "Barricades."

Reload on the move if you can. Reloading on the move is a skill you need to learn, and it's not that hard once you've mastered the basics of speed reloading. You know where the gun is, and you know where the magazine is. It's just a matter of holding everything securely and putting it all together. You're better off going a bit slower and being able to reload than arriving at your firing point and having to reload there.

You don't ever want to get to the last target and have only one or two bullets in your gun. It's very easy to blow a match doing that. By the last target, you're winded and excited, and the likelihood that you'll miss is increased. Better to insert that extra magazine and go into the home stretch with the confidence of a fully stoked gun.

Basically, stay smooth and controlled. Don't get jerky with the running and don't pull the trigger before you're all set up.

* * *

Those, then, are the basics of practical shooting. Once you've mastered them, you're ready to get into the hectic world of competition. Or, if you're not interested in continuing competition, I think you're in a lot better position to defend yourself and your family in an armed encounter.

If you've learned nothing else, remember this: Front sight; squeeze the trigger.

All About Matches

The name of the game is competition, and it's a tough game. Once you've learned the basics and practiced the techniques in this book, it's time to begin match shooting.

The toughest part of match shooting is mental preparedness. Given two shooters of equal (or nearly equal) skill, the winner will be determined by the shooter who is best prepared in his or her mind. In a way, good mental preparedness is a cross between having a positive mental attitude and absolutely fanatical single-mindedness—this *is* my sport, and I *will* excel—but that's not all.

Good mental conditioning is hard to explain. Some shooters have the mistaken idea that they can think their way into winning without the hours and hours of practice. Conversely, I know of shooters who practice for hours on end, only to be defeated by their bad mental attitude. If you're going to win in a match or survive on the street, positive attitudes and practice must go hand in hand.

The first step to good mental conditioning is to have a game plan, a goal. From the beginning of my professional shooting career, my goal was to be the best, to be a champion. Everything I did in shooting was aimed toward that goal. Along the way, though, I think I discovered a more important goal. I discovered that the only person you should ever compete with is yourself, and the goal should be to be the best you can. I found that in a match, if I had done my best, I could always go home a winner. If I hadn't done my best, even the biggest victories were sour. In the 1980 Bianchi Cup I did so poorly that I couldn't even speak to my wife for two weeks after the match. I had lost sight of my goal and had gone out there to show everybody how *bad* I was. The next match was the IPSC Nationals, and I decided that the Nationals would determine whether I stayed in shooting or not. My sole goal in the Nationals was to prove to *myself* that I could shoot. I won the IPSC championship.

My first recommendation on mental conditioning, then, is to never forget what the goal is. If your only goal in going into competition is to beat John Shaw or Mickey Fowler or Ross Seyfried you've already lost.

After you have your goal, you need a game plan for your day-to-day shooting. But you have to be careful not to make your day-to-day goals so high that you become discouraged. As an extreme example, if you just started shooting IPSC, it's unreasonable to imagine you're going to win next year's Bianchi Cup. Not that the

Notice hands are shoulder high and no more.

Bianchi Cup isn't something worth striving for, but your day-to-day goals should be within reach. Your first month's goal might be to place highly in the local club match. The next month's goal might to be to *win* the local club match. Next, aim yourself at the regional and statewide matches. Then go for the Bianchi Cup or national championship.

You should have goals in your practices, too. Can you get 25 percent faster in your one-shot draws? Can you knock down 25 plates in a row in timed fire? The good thing about establishing goals is that it gives you a method for monitoring your progress. You know where you stand at any given time, and you know how far you've got to go. You want to be honest with yourself and your evaluations of your shooting in your practice. If you're not progressing as fast as you think you should, talk to other shooters about it, especially if you know shooters who are better than you. When I've got a problem, I don't hesitate to pick up the phone and call one of the people I shoot with for help and advice. Conversely, seldom do two days go by when I am not called by a shooter looking for advice. I think that is one of the things that makes the sport of practical pistol shooting special. We work together, and it advances the sport.

One of the reasons I recommend practicing with another person so highly is that it's easier for two people to keep each other's spirits up. Sometimes solitary practice begins to resemble a Chinese water torture.

Another aspect of mental conditioning is the ability to think through a course, shot by shot and step by step. I cannot emphasize too highly how important this is! You should *never* just breeze in and shoot a match; that's a guaranteed way to lose. The way to win at a match is to plot the whole thing through in your mind. Run the course in your mind over and over, even if it's a simple stand-up shoot.

What I try to do is break every match down into its component parts. As I explained in the section on "Assault Courses," I want to know in advance where my feet have to go and what my hands have to do. I want to block out each shot in my mind. It sounds too simple, but I have lost matches because I forgot to "lock in" a shot in my head. Practical matches are very fast, and sometimes you don't have a chance to think it all out while the match is running. If you've pre-programmed your movements and your shots, you don't *have* to think it out. It's already there.

A good example was at last year's World Shoot in South

U.S. Nationals 1982 hostages everywhere with white stripes. Holler duck and start shooting. Hoping they all hit the dirt.

When I'm working as Rangemaster on my own range, my word is law. Always obey the rangemaster's instructions.

Africa. In one of the events, the competitors had to jump off the back of a truck. But they had to do so with their guns holstered, which, when they were moving as fast as they were, was not a natural reflex. One member of the American team was almost disqualified for failing to holster his gun. The way to handle an obstacle like that is *before* the match when you're blocking everything out. Think, "After my last shot, I turn to the right, reholster my gun, and jump off the truck . . ." It works!

The same goes for any match. Think, "Turn right, shoot the far target, turn left, shoot the stop plate . . ." or whatever the course calls for. It also helps to focus the mind—I like to have ten minutes or so to myself before a match, and that's what I'll be doing in that time. I take it shot by shot, and in addition to programming my mind, I'm clearing it of other distractions like the crowd around me or the prize table a few feet away.

I'd like to say that such concentration is a sure-fire cure for match nerves, but there is no such thing. Nobody shoots as well in competition as they do in practice, which is why a tough practice regimen is so important. Match pressure always nibbles away at your score, and the only way to beat it is to shoot lots of matches. It's unusual for a new shooter to do well in national shoots the first year (although there are exceptions), and the reason is that the shooter first has to learn to cope with match pressure.

You need to learn to ignore the audience, and I know that's a hard trick to learn. Sometimes I can't screen out the audience, and I've been shooting professionally for four years. The more people you shoot in front of, though, the easier it becomes.

Another thing you want to *avoid* is spending a lot of time around the prize table trying to figure out what you can win. I know a lot of shooters who actually carry a list of the prizes in their pockets. The shooters who carry those lists seldom win anything listed on them, either. It just adds an unnecessary pressure that you *don't* need. The first year I shot, the first place I went was to the prize table, then to the scoreboard, to see what score I could beat, and if I beat it, what could I win. The best shooters aren't worried about the prize list or the scoreboard, I finally learned. They're out there just to survive every day, try to avoid making any stupid mistakes, and do the very best they can do. That's the biggest tip in this book, too. Try to be the best you can be.

When you go to a match, you want already to have tested your equipment and to know that it works. You've charged all your match magazines and run all your match rounds through the gun.

1982 IPSC Nationals going over wall in Modified Cooper Assault. Remembering not to hit top bar - 10 second penalty if you knock it down.

U.S. Nationals 1982 Basic Match. Note 2 shooters on line.

A good tip here is to number your practice and your match magazines. When you have a jam that's not ammo related, make a note of which magazine it is. If you have more than a couple of jams in the same magazine, throw it away. As I said earlier, magazine technology has a long way to go. You always want to buy the best for your match magazines, too. Again, I recommend the Bill Wilson-Bill Rogers custom combat magazine for matches. The one-piece military magazines, if they work in your gun, are fine for practice.

You'll have already made sure that your empty magazines fall from your gun and that the slide stop holds the slide open after the last shot.

Watch how the firing line is being run before you go up to shoot. You don't want to be in a position where you hold up the shoot and have the range officer speak to you. It breaks your concentration. You want everything to go smoothly when you step up to the line.

When the shooting starts, follow your game plan exactly. More matches are lost by shooters who decide to make some last minute changes in a match they'd carefully thought out. In most cases, your careful pre-planning, thinking each shot out, will serve you better than a last-minute change.

Another thing you want to avoid, especially in a several-day match, is tinkering with your equipment between matches. A good example of this is cleaning your gun every night. No top shooter that I know of, myself included, cleans the gun every night of a match. You might wipe the gunk out of it, but do not strip it down and clean it thoroughly. The reason is that a good cleaning just might alter the way the gun shoots. For sure it's going to alter the first (or even first few) shots until the bore is clear and dry.

What I like to do is shoot a gun a thousand or more times in practice before I clean it. Then, several days before the match, I take it completely apart, clean it thoroughly, and inspect each part of the gun for damage, wear, or any other sign that breakage is imminent. I then reassemble the gun and shoot it in practice for several more days *without* cleaning it again. I won't clean the gun again until after the match.

Also, resist any temptation to make a "few minor changes" in the gun at the match. I've given in to that temptation myself. After all, some of the top gunsmiths in the country come to these matches, and it seems like such a shame not to let them correct a few little things. DON'T DO IT! Even the smallest change can alter the way the gun shoots and cost you the match. Do all your tinkering between matches. In fact, I usually don't like to let other shooters handle (or fool with) my competition gun before a match. All they've got to do is drop the slide on an empty magazine, and there goes the trigger pull.

As my good friend and holstermaker Gordon Davis says, equipment includes not only your gun and leather. It also includes your ear and eye protection, the hat you wear to keep the sun out of your eyes, even the clothes you wear to the match. All this ancilliary equipment needs to be checked as well. I once bought a new hat and went to a match, only to have the hat's bill bend down and block my vision during an assault course! Check everything!

Wear loose, comfortable clothes and a good pair of sneakers or running shoes.

Another important match tip is to, whenever possible, get to the match far enough in advance to practice on that course. I never shoot as well away from home as I do on my own range—I don't think there's a person who can shoot as well as I can on my home turf—that's the home court advantage. Before you go to a match, find out as much as you can about the match. What courses will you be shooting? When will you be shooting them, and where will the sun be? Set up each of those courses at your home range if you can (if you're a member of a club, shoot some club practice matches with the same course and same rules as the big match). DO NOT BURN YOURSELF OUT IN PRACTICE! This is one of my worst failings. I'll practice too hard and peak too soon. By the time I get to the match, my best scores are behind me. If there's a particular course that you seem to be having trouble with, skip it and go on to another. Then come back to the troublesome course of fire on another day.

If you arrive at a match slightly before it's scheduled, hopefully you can get a chance to practice there (probably not on the actual course). This is very important. I've seen a lot of shooters drive up to a match, get out of the car and go shoot. I've never seen a shooter score well doing that. When money is tight, try to find another shooter to share expenses. Don't be afraid to call a shooter who's organizing the match and ask where is the closest cheap motel—practical shooting is hardly the sport of millionaires! Fellow shooters will understand the problem.

Modifying the Handgun

Let's assume that you've just bought a Government Model .45 and you want to set it up for IPSC-style shooting. What do you need to have done to the gun?

That's a question guaranteed to keep hundreds of pistolsmiths backlogged for years. The .45 automatic lends itself to dozens of modifications under the heading of "accurizing," "customizing," or just plain "dressing-up." Some of the modifications are not only good, they're absolutely necessary. Other modifications are simply ways of separating naive shooters from their money.

Another point to keep in mind is that in many cases, the number and kind of modification you make to your gun is a personal decision, dictated by your own personal needs. Is your gun to be strictly a match gun, or a gun used for self-protection as well? In some cases, the part of the country you live in can make a difference—for example, IPSC competitor Brian Enos lives in Arizona, a state with moderate gun laws and lots of wide open spaces. For his purposes, a highly modified Wilson Accu-Comp is perfectly acceptable for hunting small game and general carry—the extreme accuracy of the match gun is necessary for long-range handgunning.

Conversely, a police officer who carries a shorter .45 Commander as an off-duty gun and wants to compete with the same weapon faces a whole different set of needs, and, as a result, requires a whole different set of modifications.

In addition to my own thoughts on the subject of gun modification, I went to two of the top gunsmiths in the country for their thoughts. Neither Jim Clark of Keithville, Louisiana, nor Bill Wilson of Berryville, Arkansas, needs that much introduction. Clark's super quality match guns are acknowledged winners, whether in NRA bullseye, PPC, or combat shooting. His Bowling Pin .45 is the state-of-the-art in combat shooting, and I'm proud to say it's a gun I helped pioneer and popularize. I won both my national championships with the same Clark Pin Gun.

My other match gun comes from Wilson, and it's every bit as state-of-the-art as Clark's masterpieces. Bill Wilson is a tough IPSC competitor himself, and his shop specializes in the combat shooter. In my opinion, these two men know as much about the combat .45 as any two people in the country.

We all agree that an out-of-the-box .45 is going to need several modifications right off the bat, including sights, a new trigger and trigger job, lowering the ejection port (unless it's a Commander or a Gold Cup), and throating the barrel.

Wilson's new fixed sight for Government .45. There is none better on the market.

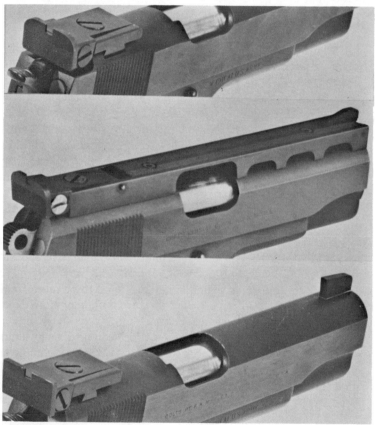

Three *Wichita sight systems — Top-combat adjustable sight* **milled** *into slide - middle - rib. Model made to fit revolvers or* **auto's** *— bottom-adjustable sight that can be installed direct-ly into factory dove tail without any milling required with replacement front.*

The issue sights on a .45 Government Model are awful, a situation that, for some reason, Colt has steadfastly refused to change. The issue sights are too small, are very hard to pick up, and are, in my opinion and the opinion of practically everyone else in the shooting industry, totally worthless.

You'll need a new front sight as well. As discussed earlier, most top shooters use a black front sight without any colored insert. In fact, I use a carbide lamp to smoke my sights black before each match. I prefer an undercut post front sight because a ramp tends to reflect sunlight. If your gun is a duty gun, however, or one to be carried on the street, you should go with a ramp front to facilitate drawing the gun from a holster. The front sight should be silver-soldered in as well as staked. A front sight just staked in, says Jim Clark, is not going to stand up to the kind of punishing shooting an IPSC shooter routinely does.

The next step up from a fixed sight is an adjustable sight. I prefer adjustable sights on all my guns because I shoot a variety of loads, and each load has a different point-of-impact. It's a simple matter to adjust the sights to fit the load. If you plan to be shooting a number of loads, adjustable sights are the way to go. The drawback to adjustable sights is that they tend to be more fragile than their fixed counterparts, and they are definitely more expensive to purchase and have installed.

A typical fixed-sight installation, which can be done by almost any local gunsmith, will probably not run over $50, including the cost of the sights. Adjustable sights require precise milling of the slide for a proper fit, and the cost will generally be double that of fixed sights.

There are several factors to take into consideration when selecting adjustable sights for the .45. A number of adjustable sights are available that slip right into the existing sight dovetail. Most of these sights are not suitable for combat use because they position the sights too high, where they are exposed to too many

These .45s are from Bill Wilson's shop, At the top is one of his basic combat conversions; below that, his top-of-the-line Accu-Comp.

New from Wilson • Accu-Comp "LE" Master Grade with Metaloy finish. Below is Jim Clark's top-of-the-line Bowling Pin Gun, my main competition weapon with Metaloy finish.

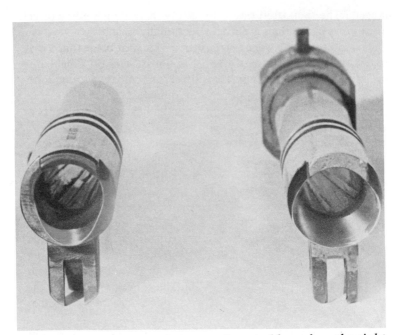

Above is a comparison of an over throated barrel on the right with a stock barrel on the left. Note how much metal has been removed to guarantee consistent feeding. I do not recommend quite this much but one should get the idea. Magazines should have base pads to make insertion easier. Pictured are two take-down Wilson-Rogers magazines with built-in pads and rounded followers.

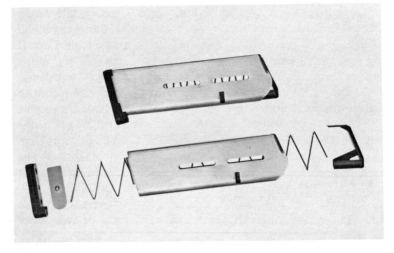

dangers. The sight itself has to be sturdy, because it's going to get much more usage than a duty sight normally would.

In addition, you want a sight with a wide, flat blade that's easy to pick up quickly. As we discussed in our chapter on "Sight Picture," one of the most important aspects of combat shooting is being able to pick up your sight picture quickly.

The sight should be "melted," that is, have no sharp edges or protrusions that can hang on clothing or snag in any way.

I recommend the Wichita, a low-mount adjustable sight, which undoubtedly is the upcoming sight in combat competition. It is readily available from most top gunsmiths (both Clark and Wilson offer it, with installation, for approximately $100), it meets all the criteria listed above, and is, generally, a tough sight to beat.

A second alternative is the new Wilson sight, which does mount in the existing dovetail but features a relatively low profile. I have been shooting one of the new Wilsons on my Bowling Pin gun and have been impressed with this sight. It features an excellent sight picture with the advantage of not requiring any milling on the slide. The sight is inexpensive, there is a big savings on the installation, and it can probably be installed locally.

I do *not* recommend milling an S&W K-frame revolver sight into the slide of a .45, as was all the vogue in combat circles a few years back. Although this is definitely the most "finished" looking installation, the S&W sight just does not offer the broad, flat sighting surface of a Wichita or Wilson. It is slower to pick up and not as precise in its adjustments. Add that to the fact that it costs exactly as much as the Wichita to install (and more than the Wilson), and you'll see why I suggest passing it by.

A word here is in order about Gold Cups. While target shooters around the world have sung their praises, I have never had much luck with the Elliason sights that come on the Gold Cup. If you like them, keep them, but first replace the roll pin that's holding them in! Regardless of what you read in gun magazines, the Elliason sight will fly off because of the flimsy pin. One day, in a fit of disgust, I drilled through the hole on my Gold Cup sights with a size-larger drill bit, and then broke the drill bit off in the hole. That solved the problem permanently! I brought the problem up to Colt recently, and also told them about my "solution." The front sight on a Gold Cup is also only staked on. The first time it pops off, have it soldered back by a competent gunsmith.

The next step is usually the trigger. I know of very few people who like the stock short trigger on the .45. I know of even fewer

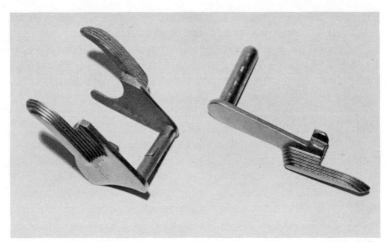

Above is an ambidextrous safety (left) and an extended slide release by Armond Swenson. The photo below shows the details of Jim Clark's Bowling Pin Gun barrel set-up. Note the absence of a bushing on the Pin Gun.

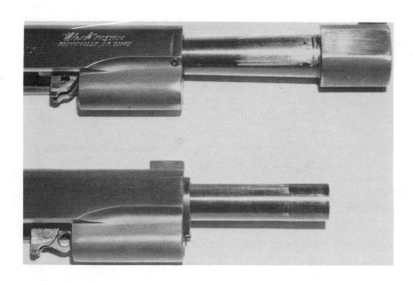

people who can stand the super-heavy trigger pulls that have been turning up on production guns recently. A good trigger job and a new longer trigger are, I think, necessities. Long triggers are available from both Clark and Wilson.

We briefly touched earlier on the question of trigger pulls, and I think it's important to mention them again. On a match gun, you want the lightest trigger pull you can get. A trigger pull that light, in order to be safe, requires the tuning of a master pistolsmith, like Wilson or Clark. A good, clean pull of two or two-and-a-half pounds is attainable on a match gun.

Such a light pull is NOT desirable on a gun that might serve double duty as a self-defense weapon or a duty weapon! For the double duty gun, the trigger pull should be between three-and-a-half and four-and-a-half pounds, and under no condition should the hammer follow the slide down!

The same sort of situation applies on the trigger stop, a screw set into the trigger to prevent overtravel. Yes, definitely, on a match gun, but never on a street gun.

One modification that's a necessity on both street and match guns is throating—polishing the feed ramp and enlarging the throat area of the chamber to allow it to feed other than hardball ammo. The .45 auto was designed to feed military full-metal-jacket round nose ammo only, and lead bullets, especially lighter weight lead bullets, and non-round nosed designs tend to hang up on the feed ramp or going into the chamber in some guns. Throating is the way to cure that problem. The amount of throating varies from gunsmith to gunsmith. I usually throat my guns myself, and I throat them extensively (see photos). I've never had any problems with my throated guns, and they'll feed anything.

You will need a speed safety of some sort. The issue safety on a .45 works well for some people, especially for street use, but most shooters prefer an extended safety of some sort. They're quicker and more positive than the standard safety, and you don't have to reposition your grip to use the safety.

I think an ambidextrous safety is nice, but not necessarily vital. It is handy for weak-hand matches, where you can use your weak-hand thumb to punch off the safety, and if you're a lefty, the ambidextrous safety is absolutely necessary.

I recommend either the Swenson extended safety or the M-S Safari Arms safety. Both offer right-hand only or ambidextrous sets. In most cases, it is better to have the safeties fitted by a pistolsmith.

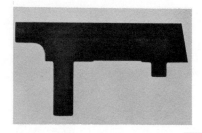

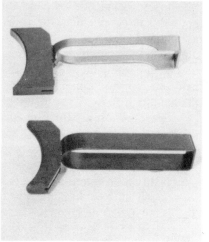

At top left is a Wilson extended ejector. The only drop in on the market. At the top right is a pair of triggers, one short (the lower) and one long. I recommend a long trigger for a .45 in most cases. Below are examples of two grip safeties, a regular Colt on the left and the beavertail grip safety manufactured by Wilson-Clark on the right. The Wilson-Clark grip safety is by far the best type to use, as explained in the text.

One item I think is invaluable is the Wilson-Clark beavertail grip safety. While there are a number of "beavertail" style grip safeties now available, Wilson-Clark is by far and away the best designed. With it installed on your gun—and it has to be installed by a pistolsmith as some of the frame has to be ground away—your hand slides right into position when you grip the gun in its holster. During recoil, the beavertail grip safety seems to distribute the recoil better, allowing you to come back on target quicker. It works so well, in fact, that when I first started using one, my scores improved 10 percent. I now have them fitted on all my match .45s.

Another recommended modification is beveling the magazine well to make insertion of a new magazine easier. I now use and recommend the Shaw Speed•E•Load, a funnel that fits over the magazine well and makes loading even easier. It's one of those "better mousetrap" ideas that really works, and at approximately $30.00, it's a bargain.

One standard modification that both Wilson and Clark recommend is checking, or in some cases, replacing—the ejector; also polishing and adjusting the extractor. I use a long ejector in all my match guns and accept the trade-off of positive ejection over ease of dropping a loaded round, as discussed in our chapter on "Clearing Jams." I recommend a long ejector (or an ejector from a Commander, which is slightly longer than a stock model) in match guns. Bill Wilson makes a long combat ejector.

The extractor should grip the case firmly, but not so firmly that it's hard to slip the case out from under it. I recommend bending your extractor slightly, replacing it in the slide, and making sure that it grips the cases properly with at least four pounds of pressure.

On a Government Model, the ejection port itself should be lowered to allow the ejected cases clearance. This is a very idiosyncratic point with guns—some require cutting away more metal than others. Once you have the basic job done, if you have any other ejection problems, call your pistolsmith and discuss those problems with him.

The grips are another area of controversy. For street use, one of the best grips available is the Pachmayr rubber grips. I use them on some of my revolvers, and when I began competition, I used them on my match guns. I noticed that none of the top shooters used them. The problem seems to be that Pachmayrs get slippery when wet with sweat, and in the course of a day's shooting, your hands are going to sweat.

As a result, I changed back to stock Colt grips, which are

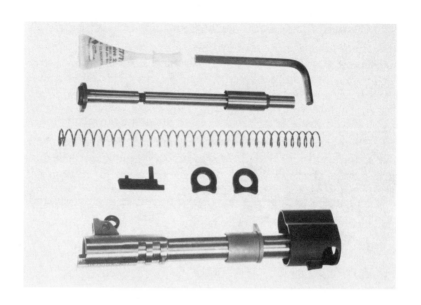

(Above) Wilson Combat Accu-Comp II Drop-In Kit. (Below) Introducing the Shaw Speed•E•Load, the best inexpensive magazine well on the market. Made of stainless steel and designed for all 1911 model Colts.

sharply checkered over their entire surface. I have the front part of the frame and the mainspring housing checkered or stippled, depending on who does the work. Jim Clark's stippling works very well because it's *sharp*, like trying to hold a wood rasp. Wet or dry, though, your hand does not slip! Bill Wilson does an extraordinary job of hand-checkering on the front of the frame. It's beautiful as well as functional.

There are some things we *don't* recommend. For a start, if you use my grip, there's no need for squaring the front trigger guard or any checkering or stippling of the guard because your finger's not going to be up there. Save some money and forget it.

Pass any ambidextrous slide release or, in fact, any extended slide release at all. "You won't see any serious shooter with an extended slide release," says Bill Wilson. "Sometimes the added weight of such a release will cause it to pop up and lock the gun up in mid-cycle. If you've absolutely *got* to have one, Safari Arms makes the best."

If you can afford it, I highly recommend that you take your stock gun out of the box and send it to either Wilson or Clark and let them set your gun up for you.

With Clark, ask for the basic Combat Conversion, which includes:

Accuracy job
Trigger job
Low-mount Bo-Mar or S&W sights
Stippled front strap
Altered feed ramp (throating)
Lowered ejection port
Beveled magazine well

With Wilson, specify the #110 Basic Combat Pistol, which includes:

High visibility fixed sights
Extended combat safety
Trigger job with long trigger
Beveled magazine well
Polish feed ramp and throat barrel
Polish and adjust extractor
Lower ejection port
Heavy duty recoil spring

The basic Clark job is $360 on your gun; the #110 Wilson job is a steal at $165. A more comprehensive Wilson job, equivalent to

Ed Brown at work in his shop. Ed is a newcomer to the competition gun market. He makes a real fine gun with a recoil reduction system that's as good as any, and better than most.

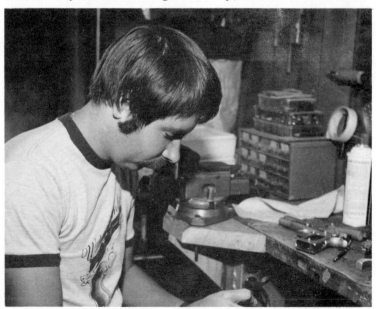

Bill Wilson at work in his shop in Berryville, Arkansas.

the Clark, runs $370 with low-mount Bo-Mars. The basic Clark accuracy job is $168.30.

The advantage to doing this all in one shot is that your gun will be ready to go when you get it back. If there are any problems at all, both men will unconditionally stand by their work. You know what you're getting, and you can depend on it.

Before we leave the topic of gun modifications, I want to look at the two fine top-of-the-line match guns, the Clark Bowling Pin and the Wilson Accu-Comp. Both guns are similar in that they have a shroud, or weight, extending beyond the front of the slide. In the case of the Clark, it's actually a weight screwed onto a threaded six-inch National Match barrel and epoxied in place. In the Accu-Comp, Wilson uses a five-inch barrel with a one-inch extension expansion chamber on the front of the barrel.

"The pressure starts subsiding when the bullet leaves the muzzle," Wilson says, "which causes a slight delay in unlocking. The ejection of the spent round is much more positive with an expansion chamber."

The Accu-Comp conversion also utilizes a recoil guide rod that holds the barrel up during the recoil cycle, which Wilson credits with making the gun reliable.

The six-inch barrelled Bowling Pin Gun was originally designed for Colt executive Lew Sharpe in 1979 to use on bowling pins. I saw it at the Bianchi Cup match in 1979 and literally fell in love with it. I ordered one in September, and it's still the best match gun I've ever used. The longer sight radius and the extra recoil control gives the competitive shooter the edge he really needs to win.

"The thing that makes the combat shooter so tough to build a gun for is that the types of shooting are so different," says Clark.

Either the Pin Gun or the Accu-Comp are amazingly versatile for match guns, and I use them in all sorts of competition, plus some small game hunting. I highly recommend them.

Ed Brown has come a long way as a competitor with his new gun. In 1983 he finished 9th in IPSC Nationals; 13th at the Bianchi Cup; and 15th in the World Championship. He now makes a short Maxi-Comp (¾ inch shorter than his standard model) which makes it a faster pointing gun. I've found no accuracy loss with his compensators.

Combat Leather

When you get right down to it, leather is one of the most important aspects of shooting, whether it's in competition or on the street. The number of both holster manufacturers and types of holsters seems to be multiplying these days. A quick flip through any gun magazine will turn up a staggering variety of holsters, from fancy western rigs to tiny shoulder holsters, all guaranteed to be safe, secure, snatchproof, concealable, revolutionary, traditional and all sorts of other claims.

A good holster—*any* good holster—has two basic functions: to hold the gun secure and to free it when you need it. Above all, the gun needs to be as accessible as possible. If you can't get to the gun when you need it, what's the use of having the gun in the first place? That especially applies to people who must carry a gun—haven't you ever wondered how an undercover police officer in tight jeans was going to get his Chief's Special out of his ankle holster? The answer is, of course, that he's *not* going to get it out quickly in a surprise encounter.

Ideally, you want a holster that can be drawn with either hand. In our type of practical competition, this is absolutely necessary. Weak-hand shooting is, as we've seen, a basic part of IPSC competition. On the street, being able to reach your gun with your weak hand if your strong hand has been injured could be a matter of life and death.

A holster also needs to hold the gun securely. Simple as that idea sounds, it has only been in recent years—and under pressure from competitive shooters—that many holster makers have risen to the challenge and produced holsters that allowed access while, at the same time, providing security. Security is, of course, a consideration on the street as well as at a match. One of the most concealable (and probably one of the oldest) ways of carrying a small revolver is to just stuff it in your waistband. The old cop trick of wrapping a few rubber bands on the grips to keep the gun from sliding works, too, but it's hard to beat a set of rubber Pachmayr grips for holding a revolver in place. I have also bounced my favorite Chief's Special off the floor via a pants leg. An unpleasant feeling, I assure you. Security counts.

For the combat shooter, security is crucial. The gun has to stay in the holster through all sorts of battering, yet be available for a quick draw. What you're talking about is spending $100 - $125 for a good holster ring, and when I heard that when I was first starting out, I thought everyone was crazy. Even $85 was unheard of (at least, to me.) I figured I could go down to the local gunstore and buy a holster for five or six dollars—and get a pretty good holster to boot!

I was getting ready for my first big match, and I didn't want to buy one of these super-expensive holsters. I took my own advice and went out and bought a Bucheimer holster, one of the old spring-loaded crossdraws where the gun pulled out from the rear. Then I took a razor blade and cut the whole *front* out of it! That put the spring tension back on the trigger guard, and that was just super. With a "break-open" front, you could just whip that gun out, like a PPC gun.

The first big match I ever went to was in Berryville, Arkansas, the 1979 Midwest Championship. I'd never seen any top-notch IPSC shooters work out, but Ray Chapman was going to be there; Raul Walters was going to be there; Jerry Usher was going to be there; Nick Pruitt from California was going to be there. It was probably best that I *didn't* know what I was getting into.

I was out practicing the day before the match when Ray Chapman came over and, taking one quick look, demanded to know who did my leatherwork. I still think what caught his eye was the red velvet lining I'd glued in the little Bucheimer to "slick it up." I still figured I just didn't have the money for one of those expensive rigs.

To make a long story short, I beat Ray Chapman by one-tenth of a second. Then Bill Wilson, the Arkansas gunsmith who was hosting the match, beat *me* by a tenth of a second. That was Bill's first big shoot, too. We couldn't believe we'd both beaten the reigning world champion.

Later that afternoon I met Californian Gordan Davis, who was at the match to promote his popular but expensive holsters. Since I'd come in second in the match and won a $500 pistol, I figured I was rich enough to buy a "real" holster. I gave Gordon the incredible sum of $42 for a holster. I've still got the Bucheimer, though, and the red velvet is holding up pretty well.

I've still got the original holster I bought from Gordon, and that holster has been *used*. It looks pretty well worn from the outside—I never have cleaned it or put any oil on it—but it doesn't have Thread One broken. There are no cracks in it, no splits in the leather. This season, I'm letting a good friend use it in IPSC competition.

I use a crossdraw rig. The reason I use a crossdraw, as opposed to a high-riding hip holster, is that *I've* found the crossdraw to be a little faster and easier to work with the weak hand. In terms of flat-out speed, a hip holster is no faster or slower than a crossdraw,

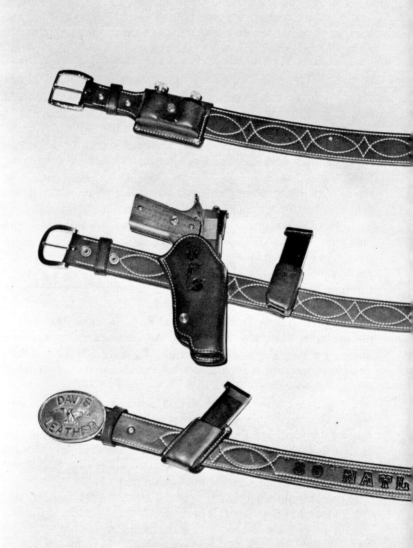

A selection of combat leather

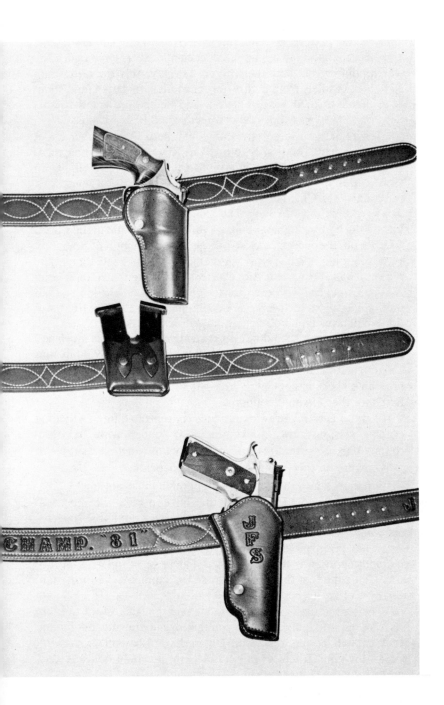

something I've proved to myself using a timer.

The secret to speed is not having a trick holster, something I've emphasized to the various law enforcement officers I've taught. It's worth pointing out here that Bill Jordan, arguably the fastest gun alive, works solely from a *duty* holster of his own design (and widely available through retail outlets), and he can draw and fire his Smith and Wesson Model 19 in something like .27 of a second!

There are two important things you need to remember about combat leather. The first is to buy the very best. Sure, it's expensive, but it's going to last almost forever. It's no different from your gun. If you want to be a serious competitor, or you want to see to it that your Chief's Special doesn't end up on the floor at an awkward time, buy the best. The second thing to remember is that buying the best isn't going to make you the fastest gun in the world. Speed from the draw is, as I've said before, a function of how fluid your motion is. When you waste motion, you waste time. The reason I was able to beat Ray Chapman with the red velvet special is that I *practiced* with that holster until my arm ached. I worked until my draw was as *simple* as I could make it—a single, fluid motion. Whatever type holster you buy, *practice* with it.

I will confess that I don't practice my draw nearly as much as I practice my shooting. I know hotshots who can really whip that gun out of the holster and miss a shot at seven yards. The old lawman's cliche is applicable here—it's not the first shot; it's the first shot that *hits* that counts.

I try to keep my drawing practice concentrated into fairly long evening sessions now, drawing my .45 loaded with DUMMY rounds 100 - 200 times just to remind my arm where it's supposed to go. More on this in our section on Practicing.

What goes into the making of a good combat holster?

There are a couple of things that have to be taken into consideration when building a combat holster, and I think that the fact that I am a shooter—and the fact that I'm not afraid to ask questions—has given me a lot insight into those considerations. The first consideration is that the shooter has to get a full grip on the gun. That's the first thing to look for. The minute you go for your gun, you've got to be able to get a full grip on it.

The second major consideration is that the front of the holster has to be cut low enough to give you the edge in drawing, but has to retain enough tension to keep the gun in. No holster will retain your gun all the time. It's just not possible. But it should hold the gun *most* of the time.

The design of the holster I use was put together in the summer of 1977 for Jerry Usher, one of the first five team mebers to represent the United States in international IPSC competition. Usher decided on a crossdraw because of the way matches were begun—with the hands together at the center of the body. A crossdraw holster gave a little margin on speed.

If anything, crossdraws now are even more popular than they were then. They're safe when you draw with the weak hand. At no point in the draw does the gun engage any part of your body.

The better holsters use a slightly heavier-weight leather than ordinary (6/22 of an inch thick versus 5/32 of an inch), and I can attest to the fact these holsters hold their shape excellently. Like most practical holsters for competition, the crossdraw features a tensioning screw on the rear to adjust the amount of tension holding the gun in.

One of the things to put into a good holster is simplicity. When you get too many mechanical things in a holster, something happens. It's Murphy's Law working. The same applies to the sight channel which is molded into the holster.

The newest generation of holsters (and holster makers) has come about as a direct result of the rigors of competition, a good example of how practical competition can help provide benefits to shooters at large.

Look at practical pistol shooting like car racing. If you want to find out the best car and the best driver, watch the circuit. As long as you keep your tests practical, you'll evolve equipment that works best.

For fast-draw artists in days past, the looser the holster, the better. The gun practically *fell* out of the holster as soon as it was touched. IPSC shooting has changed all that.

"We've even changed a number of our designs for police duty use," says Bill Rogers, who recently had one of his holster designs adopted by the Florida Highway Patrol. "We no longer promote front-break holsters the way we used to. A front-break puts you in a natural hip-shooting position, whereas a top-draw holster is more compatible to the Weaver position used both in competition and increasingly in police firearms training."

It all starts with the draw. IPSC shooting actually threw a challenge out to the holster industry, and they have done pretty well.

We've recently gone through (and, to an extent, are still going through) a lot of controversy in the IPSC over concealable holsters.

A segment of the IPSC would like to see all holsters used for competition to be completely concealable under street clothes and comfortable for day-long wear.

The argument for this is that the whole rationale of the International *Practical* Shooters Confederation is the word "practical;" guns and gear, including holsters, should be directly applicable on the street. For the most part, I think we're a lot closer to that ideal than most other shooting sports. The argument against the concealed holster idea is that, realistically, there aren't that many concealed weapons' permits available to the general public, and secondly, that the advances in the sport come from the constant experimentation.

My own opinion is that top guns are going to be top guns—I don't care if everyone wears their guns on top of their hats at the beginning of the match. Sometimes I think that too many people use something like a concealability rule as an excuse for their own inability to shoot well—I've seen it happen too many times. The bottom line is that when you get the gun out of the holster, you're back on even terms. Holsters are a big advantage, but they're not going to make a difference in who the top shooters are. Shooting skill is what makes the difference.

I think there's room in this sport for all kinds of people. Bill Rogers, himself a solid IPSC competitor and Florida state champion in 1981, has suggested separate events for concealable weapons and for unlimited. "There's room enough for all of us here," he says. "But I'm hoping that we won't eventually end up like the police PPC shooters. Remember, that started out as 'practical' shooting, too."

What this whole controversy has hung on, of course, is a working definition of "concealable." That definition changes depending on your size, weight, the clothes you wear, your gun—everything. I'm a pretty big guy, and, for me, a Government Model in my crossdraw rig is pretty close to concealable. As far as comfort, I've spent all day bouncing around on an all-terrain vehicle hunting while wearing my competition gun and rig. Let a five-foot, 95-pound woman try to do the same thing, though, and it's an entirely different story. Concealability becomes a judgement call, and it's tough to run a fair competition that hinges on a judgement call.

In the meantime, I think more "concealable only" matches are a good idea, and if you carry a gun on the street, by all means try

Rogers front break adjustable magazine pouch.

competing with the gun and holster you carry. In fact, I'd recommend competing with *several* different styles of concealable holsters, and carry your gun in the one that works best for you.

Reloading

You're probably already familar with the idea of reloading your own ammunition as a way of saving money. For the serious combat shooter, reloading is not just a good idea, it's a financial necessity. The over-the-counter cost of 50 rounds of .45 ammunition is pushing $20, and even military-spec hardball from the Philippines, not noted for its accuracy, is over $200 per thousand.

If you're going to shoot the amount of ammunition that is necessary to become a really excellent shot and you don't have a very rich uncle somewhere, plan on reloading your ammunition.

The combat shooter has a different set of reloading problems to face. While working up a tack-driving load for the favorite varmint rifle is actually fun, loading 500 rounds of .45 practice ammunition is not. It is incredibly time consuming, and that is time that you could be spending either practicing or with your family, who might like to see you once in a while.

My first recommendation for reloaders, then, is to bite the bullet, shell out the money, and buy a progressive reloading machine.

A progressive reloading machine is actually a small ammunition-making factory. Unlike a single-stage press, where only one operation can be done to one cartridge at a time, a progressive reloading machine produces a finished round with every pull of the lever. The more sophisticated the loader, the more rounds per hour you can load.

I use a Dillon 1000 reloader, and I recommend it highly. It's very expensive—around $2500 fully set up—but I definitely think that not only is it worth the money, but you can actually use the machine to make money as well as bullets.

I originally used an RCBS "Rockchucker" single stage reloading press, which is an excellent piece of machinery. But I found myself spending hours and hours reloading. In fact, I never saw my family at all. If it was light enough, I was practicing. As soon as it got too dark to shoot, I started reloading to get ready for the next practice session. Of course, making a living did have a way of cutting into my practice time, but that couldn't be helped. With the Rockchucker, it took me one hour to load 100 rounds of ammunition. It seemed like I could go through 100 rounds in about five minutes.

When I got the money, I went to a smaller progressive reloader, a CPM, which boosted my speed to about 300 rounds an hour. Better, but I was still spending more time reloading than shooting, and my family was still getting shorted. When I started winning some prize money, I bought the Dillon at full price, and I wouldn't take five times the price for it. I can turn out 1000 rounds in an hour, and it's easy to operate. With the automatic case feed, reloading is a snap; in just a few minutes you can produce enough ammunition to get you through an afternoon of shooting.

The Dillon was originally designed as a commercial machine, and Mike Dillon was surprised when I called him and suggested he try to sell the machines to individual shooters and clubs. Now he's heavily back-ordered. The machine's not getting any cheaper, and it's a good investment for the shooter.

If you're able to buy the big Dillon by yourself, you're in the best shape. While .38 wadcutter ammunition is fairly common everywhere, .45 reloads are not. If you live in an area where there's a lot of combat shooting activity, all the better. Using the Dillon and the sources listed in this book, you can put together 1000 rounds of .45 reloads for between $40 and $60. You can *sell* those reloads for $120 per thousand. It takes only one hour to make those 1000 rounds, so you're making a whopping $60 per *hour* with your Dillon. The machine will pay for itself in 40 hours, one working week.

The Dillon is also an extremely versatile machine—it will load .223 and .308 rifle brass as easily as .45 or .38 pistol brass. There is a large demand for .223 and .308 reloads, especially in an area where clubs are active in practical rifle shooting, or with small police departments.

My own Dillon has, in the last year-and-a-half, payed for itself many times over.

Keep in mind however, that the sale of ammunition requires a Federal Firearms License and probably a local occupational license as well. CHECK YOUR LOCAL ORDINANCES FIRST.

A combat club can do the same thing, with all the members chipping in for the purchase price. Ammunition could then be made available to club members at costs, with the outside sale of ammunition contributing to the club treasury.

If there's no way to afford the big Dillon, there is also the smaller Dillon, priced around $365. With that reloader you should be able to turn out between 300 and 400 rounds an hour, which is better than cranking away with a standard press. Many of the shooters on the IPSC circuit own the smaller Dillon and can't speak highly enough about it. It's a very reasonable price for a nominally fast machine. Both Dillons use standard reloading dies as well.

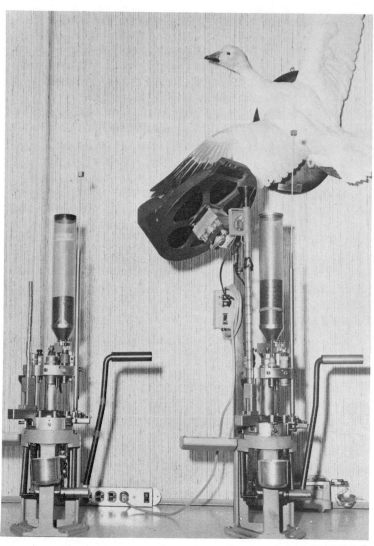

My two Dillon reloaders. One is usually set up for .45. This is definitely the finest reloader on the market. Loading not only pistol but rifle cases as well.

There are about half-a-dozen other progressive reloading machines on the market now and more on the way. Any progressive machine is better than a single press, but I've never come across a machine I liked better than the Dillon.

Once you have the machinery (or if you already have a reloading set-up), you will want to develop two loads for your gun: a light practice load and a full-house load for match or self-defense.

I strongly recommend practicing with *reduced* loads, a point of view that is not shared throughout the IPSC. I do not believe you gain anything from constantly shooting maximum loads. In fact, I think that shooting full loads all the time is a great way to develop all sorts of bad habits, not to mention extensive wear on your gun. No gun, and that includes the Government Model, was designed to be shot 25,000 or 50,000 times a year with full-house ammunition. Frames crack. Barrel lugs are deformed. Bushings shoot loose.

It's hard to develop and sustain the precision skills necessary for good shooting in the face of a heavy muzle blast and heavy recoil. That's the simple truth.

I learned this myself the hard way. While still in college, I rushed out to buy a .44 Magnum Smith and Wesson, billed, of course, as the most powerful handgun in the world. As I've said, I was pretty good plinking with a .22, so I figured the .44 wouldn't present any problems. I bought a box of hot factory loads, went down to my favorite shooting range, and quickly discovered that I had trouble hitting a 50-gallon drum! On my next snake hunt, the snakes won hands down. Every time that gun went off, I flinched. The finest handgun ever made, I thought derisively. I got rid of it because it was so inaccurate.

Later, I discovered a bullseye shooter who owned a .44 Special, and it *wasn't* that much different from a .22. I realized that the problem was never with the gun; it was with me.

Since then, I've owned a few more Model 29s, and most of the loads I shoot are .44 *Special* loads, around 800 feet per second.

Exactly the same thing goes for the .45. I have discovered that either in a match or in a hunting situation, I do not notice the added recoil or muzzle flash. I've found the same to be true with my students. If you learn how to *correctly* control a gun with light loads, you'll be able to control a gun with heavy loads.

I recommend developing a practice load somewhere in the following ranges:

Dillons economical 450 reloading press. One of the most popular reloaders of its type. Sells for $365.00 retail.

With a 200-grain lead bullet
4.0-4.4 grains Bullseye
4.7 - 5.3 grains W231

I recommend using a 200-grain lead bullet, such as the Hensley and Gibbs No. 68, sized to .001 greater than the slugged diameter of your barrel. I also recommend that you *buy* the bullets—Rogers Holster Co. in Jacksonville, Fla., offers the H&G bullets for $28 per thousand. I do NOT recommend casting the bullets yourself. Casting as many bullets as you'll need may present a health hazard because of the lead vapors. I used to cast my own bullets, and I now have abnormally high levels of lead in my body. Better to go to a commercial outfit that has all the safety precautions for bulk casting!

I like the 200-grain bullet better than the 230-grain either in lead or full-metal-jacket (FMJ), because the 200-grain doesn't recoil as hard and, generally, is more accurate (as discussed elsewhere). The exception is the 230-grain Hornady flat-nose FMJ, which is an extremely accurate bullet.

Start with the lowest load and work your way up with .1 grain increments until you find a load that is both accurate and pleasant to shoot. Don't run off more than 100 rounds of any test loading in case your gun won't shoot them accurately. Once you've got the proper load down, stick to it. There's never any reason to change, as long as your gun is unchanged. If you alter your gun, however, you may have to work up a new load. A change in the barrel bushing or a plating job can and routinely does change the point-of-aim for a specific load.

If you're shooting with fixed sights, you have the added problem of finding a load that shoots to the same point-of-aim as hardball. I suggest trying a couple of 200-grain lead bullets, say the H&G and the Hornady, and see where they shoot. If there are problems, go the Hornady flat-point and try developing a reduced load with it.

In IPSC competition, of course, you must use hardball or hardball equivalent (or hotter) loads. That's known as the "power factor," which was originally determined by a ballistic pendulum hit by a hardball bullet. The pendulum had to swing a certain amount. Once that basic standard was established, the weight of the bullet was multiplied by the velocity to get a numerical reading for the power factor. To qualify as a hardball equivalent load, the weight of the bullet times the muzzle velocity must equal the hardball power factor.

If you do not want to or have time to reload your ammo you can buy the highest quality of ammo from George Whipple at Atlanta Arms & Ammo in Lithonia, Georgia. George has loaded my match and practice ammo for all of 1982 as he has for Mark Duncan and Mike Plaxco. His ammo is the best reloaded ammo in the country. I trust them as much or more than factory. He can load them with any type of bullet and powder charge to custom meet any shooter's needs. He is also the only remanufacturer of ammo that supports our sport and my hat is off to him.

Using the same 200-grain bullet, hardball equivalent loads are:

4.8 - 5.0 Bullseye

5.9 - 6.0 W-231

Approach these and *all* loads with caution! Make sure your load qualifies before you get to a match and discover yourself disqualified. A lead bullet was allowed to be 10 percent *under* the hard-ball equivalent, but is not any more.

Another exceptionally accurate bullet designed with the IPSC shooter in mind is Hornady's new 200-grain jacketed semi-wadcutter. It is reliable and accurate in most of my guns, and I generally alternate between that bullet and the H&G No. 68 from Rogers.

A couple of other reloading tips will come in handy. Always inspect your brass *before* you load them. This is especially critical with .45 brass, because more often than not it is fired in an auto and has landed on the ground. That means that small pieces of dirt or grass could still be inside the case, even after it's been tumbled. In one particularly painful case, I lost a good bit of money in a match because of misfires. The rounds went off, but they didn't go where they were supposed to. One didn't even make it to the target. When I pulled the remainder of my bullets, I found a spider's web in one! I'd inspected the *outside* of the cases before reloading. Now I inspect the inside as well.

Also check for things like missing or badly chewed-up flash holes and cracked and deformed rims.

Be extra careful in loading your match ammunition. Shift to that ammunition and your special match magazines a few days before your match. Remember to re-zero your gun. You want to have at least one full day of practice with match ammunition and magazines to make sure there are no surprise glitches.

One tip for tumbling brass to clean it is to buy an old-type crank cement mixer. Hook up a motor if it doesn't have one, dump in about ten pounds of tumbling media, and start tumbling five-gallon buckets full of brass at the same time! It's actually cheaper than an expensive case tumbler and a lot more efficient for the combat shooter.

Finally, it's always tough finding brass. I once got a great deal on a load of .45 brass that had been shot through an old Thompson submachine gun. The reason the deal was so great was that the brass was in such bad shape that it *couldn't* be resized. Watch out for bargains that seem too good to be true. You might check to see if there's an army base or a National Guard armory nearby. Military

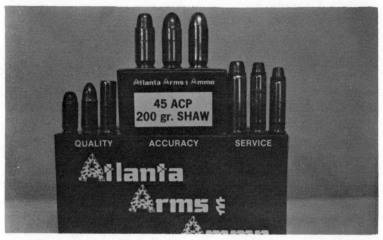

In 1982 George Whipple and myself designed a new 200 grain (on top row, left side) lead bullet that shoots very accurate and is more reliable than the sharp nosed 200 grain H&G.

Three top combat performers: (from left) The Hornady 230-grain full-metal-jacket flat-nose, the new 200-grain semi-wadcutter full-metal-jacket, designed especially with IPSC shooters in mind, and the H&G #68 200-grain lead semi-wadcutter.

---

rangemasters have to return their brass to be melted down and remanufactured, but they do so by the *pound*. If you can locate a sympathetic rangemaster, you can swap your old practice brass for once-fired military match brass, as long as the poundage is the same.

The sooner you get involved in serious reloading, the sooner you'll have more time to spend on the range shooting.

How to Practice

The most important thing about learning to practice is to first know what a good shot is. In my classes, I try to get my students to *feel* the difference between a good shot—one that goes where it's aimed—and a flyer. If their shot didn't go where it was supposed to, I want my students to be able to tell me why. you can't become a good shot until you understand the relationship between the basics—sight picture, trigger control and stance—and where your bullet goes after you pull the trigger.

I believe very strongly in the discipline of shooting groups at fairly long distances—25 and 50 yards. I do it myself, especially when I'm just beginning to practice for a specific match. Shooting groups reminds me to concentrate on the basics and shows me just how well I am concentrating. It's important to keep going back to the basics again and again, because you can *never* get so good that you can't get better.

My first recommendation for practice, then, is to spend a portion of your time shooting groups, first at 25, then at 50 yards. Only you can tell how much that proportion should be. If you're just beginning, bullseye shooting should take up most of your time until you can consistently shoot a good group, around four to five inches, at 25 yards. You can then safely adjust that proportion downward. If you are a veteran IPSC shooter reading this book to pick up a few tips, shooting groups should not occupy that much of your practice time—but you should never stop doing it!

The second practice I recommend for the practical pistol shooter is the one-shot draw, which is the most basic and most useful exercise for anyone interested in IPSC-type competition. And it couldn't be simpler.

Set up a cardboard target at seven yards and staple a standard NRA 25-yard bullseye target in the center. Move back to the firing line and, after observing all safety precautions, draw and fire one shot at the bullseye. Reholster your weapon.

The one-shot draw touches on most of the aspects of practical shooting—sight picture, trigger control, stance, grip, drawing the weapon, working the safety under pressure. Don't try to go for speed initially. The speed will come soon enough. Concentrate on doing everything correctly: Make sure your drawing motions are simple and short; make sure you have a good sight picture before you fire; make sure you know how to adjust your stance to come on target quickly.

If you've practiced all the basics and all the techniques outlined in this book, you should find your one-shot draws quickly

One-shot draws are the basic combat practice.

coming down to *under* two seconds. I've discovered that my students can get down to 1.9, 1.75 seconds after a little work. Getting down to 1.2, 1.3, 1.4 seconds, though, is *tough*, and that's the speed you're going to need to be competitive. The only way to get that speed is relentless practice.

I can't emphasize enough how much practice is actually involved. When I first started out, I went through about 600 rounds a week—much of it on one-shot draws—in practice. That doesn't take into account time spent at home in dry-firing, drawing, or reloading practice. You'll also discover that there is a speed plateau that is rough to get over. You'll seem to be stalled at that time *forever*, not getting any better. I tell my students that it's easy to get pretty good, but being *really* good is hard. My only advice is that when you hit the speed plateau, do not become discouraged. If you keep working, you can get over it.

When you're comfortable with your one-shot draws at seven yards, move back to ten yards and start the same thing over again. Do not rush this procedure! I usually don't move my students back to ten yards until they can consistently shoot "Xs" in under two seconds.

Again, concentrate on the two-inch X-ring. If you can consistently hit the X-ring from ten yards, think of how easy an eight-inch Bianchi plate is going to be. That is, in fact, the philosophy behind much of my practice. Force yourself to be better than you have to be! I have heard over and over again from shooters who should know better that, "In IPSC, you don't have to be a great shot; all you've got to do is be able to put your shots in a 10-inch circle." That's not true—all the top combat shooters in the world *are* great shots. Mickey Fowler is probably one of the greatest stand-up shooters ever. Ross Seyfried shoots 10-inch plates at 80 yards to warm up. In rapid fire match pressure, you're going to need every ace you can get. You're going to need the confidence that comes from knowing you can shoot the X-ring every time. Practice on a small target, then the big targets come easy.

Before you move out to 25 yards, though, complete this regimen first:

After you're comfortable with one-shot draws at ten yards (your time should be around two seconds), move back to the seven-yard mark, draw and fire *twice* at the bullseye. What you're working on here is your recovery time under recoil. You want each of those shots in the bullseye, as close together as possible. As you work on it, you'll eventually be able to reduce the time down to 1.5,

Above is my pop-up bank of Bianchi plates, built by Anderson Scott of Newberry Tanks, Inc., to my design. When the rope is pulled, the plates pop back up. At right is a detail of the motor of my $300 moving target. The speed can be varied by changing a rope on different pullies or by a rheostat.

1.6 seconds.

The procedure is the same: see your front sight, tighten up on the trigger, get your gun back down, and tighten up on the trigger again. Let go of the trigger, and by the time it comes back, you should have already picked up your front sight.

When you can consistently hold both shots in the bullseye quickly, back up five yards and start the exercise again, aiming for both shots in two seconds.

When you've got that down pretty well, take a piece of cardboard, three feet by six feet, put three bullseyes across in a row, four rows deep, so there are now 12 bullseyes on the cardboard.

Back up seven yards and place one shot on each of the first two bullseyes. Once you can *consistently* place both of your shots in the bullseye, start placing one shot in each of *three* bullseyes in a row. This is almost as good an exercise as the one-shot draws. Again, don't go for speed initially. Concentrate on placing each shot in the X-ring; if you *can't* place each shot in the bullseye, you're shooting *too fast*. Slow down, and concentrate on accuracy. When you're easily placing each shot in the bullseye on three targets from seven yards, move back to 10 yards.

There's not a distance limit on this sort of practice, by the way. Each time you reach a point where you can consistently hit the bullseye in a certain practice sequence, move back and make it harder on yourself. It's the same theory as using targets smaller than you can expect in a match. If you can consistently draw and fire and knock down eight-inch metal plates from 25 yards—one of my basic exercises—knocking them down at 10 yards will be a snap.

A certain portion of your practice time—not a particularly large portion—should be devoted to strong-hand/weak-hand practice. I recommend doing that practice exactly the same way, starting with one-shot draws at seven yards, then two shots on one target, then multiple targets. Practice first with your strong hand only, then your weak hand only. Remember on weak-hand draws to be extremely careful that the gun does not engage any part of your body! Again, concentrate on that bullseye and getting every shot home.

Other teachers have recommended a more extensive practice, two on three targets, then three on two targets, but I think that's a waste of ammunition. Those three practices, plus shooting groups, will exercise most of the skills necessary for practical pistol shooting.

I recommend that you always practice with a partner. It's

Two views of the plates: note the details of the level system in the bottom photograph. It's really a very simple system that can be readily duplicated by any welder or purchased directly through Newberry Tanks.

more fun, and I think you get more out of the practice session with someone watching. Whenever possible, practice with someone who is a better shot than you—the little added push of knowing what you could do helps to improve your skills faster.

One tip to make practice easier is to first understand your gun and your equipment. When I first started out practicing, I was fighting jams, fighting my gun, fighting my holster, and the results were that I wasn't getting full benefit from all the shooting I was doing. Solve your basic problems first. Make the necessary modifications to your gun, get yourself a good practical holster, find (or develop through reloading) a good accurate practice load, then grit your teeth, knuckle down, and *concentrate* on your shooting. You don't need metal targets or a sophisticated range initially—when I first started practicing for the Bianchi Cup, I used paper plates as targets.

Also remember this: After about 100-150 rounds, your shooting is probably going to go to pieces. When you see your groups start falling apart, the best thing to do is quit for the day. It's a mistake to push yourself when you're exhausted, because you're no longer learning anything and it's all too easy to become discouraged. You'll get more out of two short practice sessions where you start out fresh each day than one marathon session that leaves you a basket case.

HOMEWORK: There's a lot you can do at home to improve your shooting. Homework breaks down into three sections: drawing practice, speed reloading practice, and dry firing. Thirty minutes a night spent in homework, can translate into big increases in both speed and accuracy on the range.

The basic drills are simple, too.

1) Put on your belt and holster and practice drawing your gun, concentrating on reducing each movement to its most simple form.

2) Practice speed reloading using magazines charged with DUMMY ammunition.

3) Dry-fire your gun extensively—some competitors use a small piece of leather between the hammer and the firing pin, but I've never dry-fired a gun too much, nor have I heard of anybody who did. Pick a spot on the wall or put up a target and concentrate on getting and holding a good sight picture while you tighten up on the trigger. The gun should not move *at all*! The advantage of such dry-firing is that you get in the habit of picking up a good sight picture and correctly squeezing the trigger. Practice your one-shot draws at home, drawing, sighting, and "firing" at a target on the wall.

Don't overlook strong-hand/weak-hand practice, but don't spend a large percentage of your time on it, either.

For the serious shooter, I'd say 30 minutes a night is about right.

ADVANCED TRAINING: Once you're secure with your basic training and homework, I recommend finding the nearest practical pistol match and *compete*. Nothing sharpens the skills as much as competition. I shoot in club matches at my own range and find that to be one of the useful training sequences I have. Shooting in front of people is a good way to test how well you've really mastered shooting skills. You can quickly tell by your score just exactly where you're falling down and where you need to concentrate your practice.

For the person who must carry a gun on the street, competition shooting helps train you to shoot under pressure, and the more you shoot under pressure, the better you handle pressure. It could save your life. Match shooting also gives you a chance to "test" your street equipment and see how it stacks up against other types of guns and leather. More than one policeman I know has drastically changed his whole viewpoint on his duty equipment based on what he learned in competition.

For those of you who want to get serious about practical pistol shooting—and I hope that's most of you—my only advice is to practice even harder.

For the advanced student, I'm including a practice regimen designed by Mickey Fowler and Mike Dalton at International Shootists, Inc., in Mission Hills, California. It's a good practice sequence for the regular competitor, but should be avoided by beginners. Remember, you cannot be a great shot overnight. But you can be a great shot.

112

PRO SHOT TIMER by Competition Electronics
To become a pro requires consistant, accurate timing during practice. The Pro-Shot Timer fills this need and at the same time eleminates the need for a partner with a stop watch. Simply clip it on your belt and press the start button. After a five second delay, the beep sounds and the internal clock starts. The sound from a shot freezes the elapsed time to your last shot in the large digital display. Therefore, a precise "COMSTOCK" time to 1/100 of a second is shown. Also, the Pro-Shot Timer provides accurate professional timing for club events.

Basic Exercises

25 meters - 6 shots - prone - "Bullseye" - No time limit.

7 meters - 6 single draws - freestyle—1½ seconds (2 hands shoulder high, 2 hands clasped, and 2 hands hanging)

7 meters - 2 shots each of 3 targets - strong hand only - 5 seconds

7 meters - 2 shots each of 3 targets - weak hand only - 6 seconds

10 meters - "El Presidente" - Two on each; reload; two on each - about 10 seconds.

10 meters - 1 shot - reload - 1 shot - 5 seconds. Repeat 5 times

15 meters - 2 shots each of 3 targets - freestyle - reload - 2 shots weak hand only - 14 seconds

25 meters - 10 single draws - freestyle - 2.5 seconds
Students should decrease time elements as proficiency dictates.

"Pepper Popper"

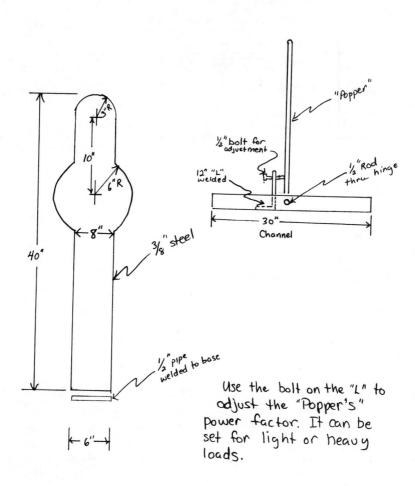

"Popper"

½" bolt for adjustment

½" Rod thru hinge

12" "L" welded

3" R

10"

6" R

8"

40"

3/8" steel

½" pipe welded to base

6"

30"

Channel

Use the bolt on the "L" to adjust the "Popper's" power factor. It can be set for light or heavy loads.

The $300 Mover

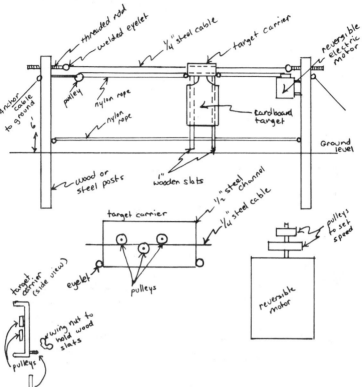

The secret of the $300 moving target set-up is an inexpensive reversible electric motor, usually available new for around $100. The motor pulls the target carrier along a steel cable via a nylon rope with one end tied to an eyelet on one side of the target carrier, the other end tied to an eyelet on the other side of the carrier. The size of the pulleys attached to the motor sets the speed of the target's movement. The target itself is stapled on two wood slats attached to the carrier with wing nuts. The target is kept vertical while moving by two nylon ropes attached to the lower part of the cable supports. The wooden slats ride between the ropes. The cable must be very tight—I had eyelets welded to a ¾ inch steel rod and used that to tension the cable.

Bianchi Plates

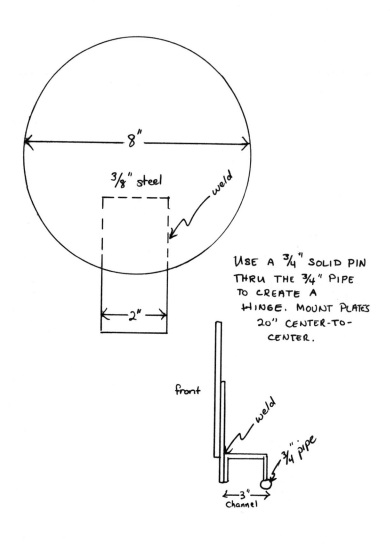

8"

3/8" steel

weld

2"

USE A 3/4" SOLID PIN
THRU THE 3/4" PIPE
TO CREATE A
HINGE. MOUNT PLATES
20" CENTER-TO-
CENTER.

front

weld

3/4" pipe

3"
Channel

The Real World

A local police department had asked me to drop in to discuss some training programs they had in mind. After a long and favorable meeting with some of the officers, they took me to meet the chief. We went through a long discussion of shooting techniques, training courses for both street and tactical teams, and range construction. Through it all, the chief only nodded every now and then. When I finished explaining how I could help in training his officers, he said, "Mr. Shaw, do you have any idea how much time and money we devote at the academy to teaching our officers *when* to shoot?" This indicated to me that how to shoot was of secondary importance.

"Sir," I replied, "you teach them when to shoot. I can teach them how to shoot." It is all too easy to confuse when to shoot with how to shoot. Proper training in both areas, with equal importance given to both subjects, is necessary for both the police officer and the armed citizen.

I am going to tell you something that might border on heresy: There is no way that I, or Ray Chapman, or even Jeff Cooper can teach you to react a certain way under fire. It cannot be done. We *can* teach you *when* to shoot lawfully; we *can* teach you *how* to shoot; we *can* even teach you *how* you *should* respond in a given situation, and, through courses like Massad Ayoob's Armed Citizen Classes, we can explain what's going to happen if you do have to go shoot. We *can* teach you accuracy, speed, tactics, and when to call your lawyer, but when it comes to the bottom line, you're going to be all by yourself. The effects of human nature make it impossible to guarantee a certain reponse for every individual who is faced with the critical situation of being under fire.

I've had some people come to me thinking they were really prepared for an armed confrontation after attending a well known school. They would back off seven yards from a target, draw their weapon and rapidly fire a group that looked like a shotgun pattern. Then they would holster their weapon and proceed to explain the difference between someone who spent all his time worrying about little metal plates and someone who is concerned with self-defense. "I mean, I've only got to hit him sort of in the middle, right? Shoot tight groups? Are you crazy?" Self-defense shooting should not become a cheap excuse for poor training or being a bad shot.

Combat pistol shooting is divided (very loosely) into two groups: the sportsmen and the martial artists. While these terms aren't totally fair because of the overlapping in techniques, they are the best we have for now. The sportsman sees competitive pistol shooting as a sport, like any other sport, the ultimate objective being to win a contest. The martial artist sees practical pistol shooting as an overture to real life, practiced solely for the possibility of an armed confrontation. In a lot of ways, I believe the distinction between the two groups is unimportant—the top shooters will be the top shooters regardless of their motivation. There is no doubt that the physical skills learned in IPSC competitive shooting can save your life in an armed confrontation.

It all boils down to a question of when and how to shoot. When to shoot is a function of strategy, good sense and the law. The laws regulating self-defense are different from state to state. Rule one is know the laws in your area. Otherwise, you may have the opportunity to learn them in a prison cell. If you haven't read Massad Ayoob's book *In The Gravest Extreme*, do so immediately. It explains the intricacies (and, in some cases, the insanity) of the laws governing self-defense. It outlines, as much as possible, the rights and responsibilities of the armed citizen. For the police officer, the situation is different and I am sure the topic is covered thoroughly in his academy training.

Strategy and good sense go hand in hand. For example, standing upright and firing away may look good on TV, but it is not good sense. The smart person looks for cover quickly. The best strategist is a "what if" person, a person who considers all the possibilities. In a sense, it is the same thought process I use before a match—think the whole course through, step by step. *WHAT IF* I step here and shoot then? *WHAT IF* I reload on the run instead of at the barricade? Sift through all the "what ifs", then mentally prepare yourself for the best course of action. When the action starts, follow that course of action as closely as possible.

Being mentally prepared works the same way in a self-defense situation. The armed encounter you will most likely face is an intruder in your home. Break this situation down into its component parts: Where did the intruder enter? Where is he likely to be in relation to yourself and family? If the confrontation is unavoidable, plan in ADVANCE all your movements and lines of fire with regard for your safety and the safety of your family and neighbors. Mental preparedness, considering the "what ifs", is a critical part of any self-defense encounter.

Good sense should also be applied in your choice of self defense weaponry. By now, the operation of the Government Model .45 is second nature to me, while another shooter may not be as comfortable with this choice. A top quality revolver is also a good selection for self-defense. I consider myself an expert shot with either of these selections, but the gun I keep by my bed is a Choate-stocked Remington 870 with a Choate magazine extension and a Nite-Site. This pump shotgun is one of the most reliable ever made—everything on it works. It may not be quite as fast as the 1100 or as small and easy to handle in close quarters as a handgun, but with proper loads it is a good-sense alternative in home protection. Good sense requires you to make the selection of what best suits your needs and abilities.

None of the above things matter if you can't shoot—more specifically, if you can't shoot under pressure. I know of no better way to learn shooting under pressure than in match competition. What match shooting teaches you is *confidence*; *confidence* in your gun and *confidence* in your ability to use it effectively. That confidence is a necessity in winning a match; it is also necessary in staying alive in an armed confrontation. To be successful in an armed confrontation, the various questions that enter your mind must be eliminated quickly and absolutely. The question of the *need* or *when* to shoot has already been answered by the circumstances of the situation. The question of *how* to shoot has been answered by the confidence received through proper training. You do not want to be in a situation where you're looking over the front sight of your gun thinking, "What do I do now?" Confidence in your weapon, abilities and mental preparation are all necessary to avoid the situation. Learning *when* to shoot is of no use, unless, first and foremost, you learn *how* to shoot.

I recently trained a number of Arkansas police officers, including a course in the combat shotgun. The first thing I told them was that regardless of what they had been told before, the shotgun was not a magic cure for the armed encounter. It is a gun, and it has to be aimed and fired. Front sight and trigger pull are still important. At the start of the course, my students seemed to believe that, "If five shots from a 12-gauge won't do it, it can't be done." I added a Choate seven-shot magazine extension and taught them to rapid-fire at multiple targets using proper techniques. Soon after the course, Officer Jimmy Smith and his partner gave chase to three bank robbery suspects. When the suspects were cornered, they didn't consider surrendering; nor did they come out of their car with nickel-plated .25 autos. They squealed to a stop with the squad car close behind, opened the doors for cover, assumed a proper Weaver stance and began firing on the officers with a .45 automatic and two six-inch .357 magnums. The squad car was literally

A photo of Officer Smith's patrol car after the shootout.

shot to pieces. Later the police estimated that almost $2,000 damage was done to the car while both officers were trapped in the front seat using their shotguns to hold the attackers off them. When the two men with magnums ran, one officer pursued them. This gave Officer Smith time to jump from the demolished car to seek better cover. At that point the gunfight had used six of his seven shots (departmental policy forbids a chambered round.) When the robber dropped the empty .45 magazine and went for a replacement magazine, Officer Smith raised up, aimed and fired. Results: one dead felon, one live police officer. I was on the range, a short distance away, and arrived on the scene shortly after the encounter. Officer Smith attributed his being alive to my previous instruction, which was a very rewarding thought for me as an instructor. Officer Smith said, "It was my last round. Although it only took a split second to line up the bead and squeeze the trigger, it seemed to take forever. Front sight and trigger pull. It saved my life."

Strategy and good sense, used with the confidence gained through proper instruction and practice, are the keys to self-defense. You must learn the *when* and *how* for handling "real world" confrontations.

The Practical Rifle

Want to get in on the ground floor of a really great new shooting sport? The hottest selling items on gun store shelves these days are the semi-auto version of military battle rifles. Springfield Armory, Heckler and Koch, Colt, Armalite, and a whole host of others offer military lookalikes, some at prices high enough to cause you to break into a cold sweat.

People buy them for a lot of reasons, from the collector's urge to own a military gun to the survivalist's urge for self-defense in *any* situation. The reason you should buy one is to shoot. The fledgling sport of practical rifle shooting is just getting off the ground. Right now there are two money shoots for practical rifle—Richard Davis' Second Chance and the *Soldier of Fortune Magazine* shoot, but I predict many more in the near future.

The reason is that practical rifle shooting is both fun and simple, and it may well be the easiest way to become involved in competitive shooting. When I showed up for my first match two years ago, I was pretty scared. I figured that the country was full of superior rifle shots—just think about the military bullseye shooters alone! They'd probably forgotten more about an M-14 than I could ever hope to know. The sum total of my training was hunting every season, and when I lay down with a borrowed M1A, those 18 X 24 inch targets three hundred meters away looked mighty small across those iron sights. I figured what the heck, "Front sight; squeeze the trigger." I shot a ten shot, four-inch group. I went on to win the 1980 *Soldier of Fortune* rifle match, coming in third the next year after giving away an incredible 200 points because of an incorrect sight adjustment. Any sport where you can still come in third, which is like kissing your sister, after messing up that bad has a lot of promise!

What you need to get involved in practical rifle shooting is a military-styled sporter and several (at least four) 20-round magazines. I highly recommend putting your money in a 7.62 Nato (.308) battle rifle rather than the U.S. 5.56 (.223) for a variety of reasons. The first is that the game tends to be scored in a major caliber/minor caliber style, like practical handgun shooting. A dead center hit with a .223 counts the same as a dead center hit with a .308, but a shot outside the bull counts three for a .223 instead of the four for a .308. A hit on the extremities of the silhouette counts one point for a .223 and three points for a .308. The other reason in the fact that the wind plays havoc with those 55 grain .22 bullets when you're shooting at any range, as was the case in last year's *Soldier of Fortune* match.

This is my excellent Springfield Armory M1A, described in the text, and a close-up of the Harris bipod.

Still, if money's in short supply you can get into the game with one of Ruger's readily available Mini-14s® or a Colt AR-15. In fact, I recommend that police who are either issued or allowed to carry a Mini-14 or an AR-15 (or even an M-16) use those guns in competition, because they'll benefit from the training. I own both Mini-14s and AR-15s, and both are good, solid guns.

When you get up into the .308 range, you're really looking at four rifles—Heckler and Koch's HK-91; the venerable Garand and the M1A, both available from Springfield Armories, and the FN-FAL. I think we can eliminate the FN-FAL right off the bat, unless you have limitless funds. That particular battle rifle can quickly approach $2000 in cash, and I've never been particularly impressed with the ones I've shot. I found their sights a little sloppy for any kind of precision shooting, although they are as close to indestructable as a rifle can be. We can also safely eliminate the Garand (unless you happen to have one lying around). If you're thinking about buying a Garand, keep in mind that for a few dollars more you can buy an M1A, which is a much more sophisticated version of the Garand anyway.

That boils it down to the HK-91 and the M1A. Let me give you a few comparative specs on them both:

The HK-91 has an overall length of 40.5 inches and weighs in at 9.75 pounds. Sights are what you'd expect on a rifle set up for combat—crude, but surprisingly accurate. The delayed roller block blowback reduces much of the recoil you might feel. The price tag is, at this writing, $656.

The M1A from Springfield is also no lightweight, tipping the scales at about 9.5 pounds. It is 44.5 inches in length and utilizes the tried and true gas-operated rotating bolt. The standard version is approximately $750.

I picked the Springfield M1A, and I'm happy with it. In fact, I think it's a great rifle.

I began shooting with the HK-91. The trigger pull on my gun was a very rough six pounds. While a six-pound pull is no disadvantage in a combat situation, it raises havoc with any sort of precision shooting. Neither I nor H-K thought it advisable to tinker with the trigger too much.

I now use a Springfield M1A. My M1A Ultra-Match has a Hart stainless steel bull barrel and a laminated zebrawood stock, plus the regular Springfield match sight. It weighs about one-third more than a standard M1A, and it will shoot one-inch groups at 100 yards all day long from a prone position with a Harris bipod. I use

Clockwise from above: The proper sequence for speed-reloading an M1A type battle rifle. Note simplicity of motion; speed-loading magazine pouch on hip.

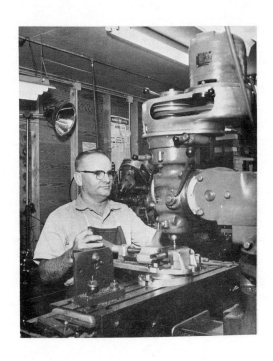

Here's the ole pro (Mr. Jim Clark) at work in his shop in Keithville, Louisiana. Mr. Clark does all types of automatic and revolver custom gunsmithing. A super nice man!

A brace of my own M1As: Top, my competition rifle in .308 caliber; bottom, a deluxe version in .243. Note slip-on rubber recoil pads.

a slip-on rubber recoil pad, and although it doesn't look pretty, when coupled with the Springfield's gas system, it reduces recoil to virtually nothing. I have never had a jam with the gun since I've been using it.

I usually hunt with a Browning semi-auto in seven millimeter with a two-to-seven Leopold scope on it. Using the scope at its seven-x setting, the best 300-yard group I can get is six to seven inches off a rest. Using the iron-sighted M1A, I can average three-inch groups at 300 yards! It's that good a gun.

They've been tinkering with the Old Garand design for a long time, and those NRA bullseye rifle shooters can do things with an M1A that you'd hardly believe possible.

The trigger pull on my M1A? About two-and-a-half crisp pounds.

Another thing that impressed me about Springfield (and H-K, for that matter) is their willingness to work with the shooters and get behind the sport. There were definitely problems with some of the M1A operating rods and housings cracking, and Springfield has assured me that the problem has been taken care of. If you have a problem with one of their rifles, they'll fix it. I'm so sure, that if you have any problems with Springfield, call *me* and I'll take it up with them. It's a shooter's company.

Another example of how they're willing to work with the shooter is in the case of bipods. *Everybody* needs a bipod—I even keep one on my XP-100 bolt-action pistol. The prone position with a bipod is the most stable position there is, and whenever there's time, in a match or hunting, it's best to utilize it. Most bipods are, however, garbage. When you put a bipod in the barrel and then put the bipod on the ground, the point of impact is going to change. The Springfield bipod was attached to the gas cylinder, which is attached to the barrel, which caused the same problem. My solution is an unquestioned recommendation for the Harris bipod. It connects to a sling swivel in the stock, solving the point-of-impact problem. As an added plus, it features very positive retraction of the legs. The representatives of Springfield saw my Harris bipod, and they were so intrigued they sent an engineer down to study my gun. As a result, they are now offering the Harris bipod installed on the stock as an option.

In fact, I was recently honored when Springfield Armory President Dennis Reese announced a "Combat Super Match" version of the M1A, set up for practical rifle shooting right out of the box.

Two versions of the Colt AR-15. The upper version is equipped with a collapsible CAR-15 stock, a Muzzle-mizer, and an Aimpoint optical sight. The Aimpoint is one of the most versatile and useful sights available.

The venerable Garand, also available from Springfield Armory (top), and the inexpensive Ruger Mini-14, a .223 rifle based on the tried-and-true Garand action. Note the similarity between the two rifles.

"We took John Shaw's rifle and his ideas and put them together in a package for the shooter," said Dennis. "The stock is beefed up to accept the Harris bipod, and it'll be offered with either a laminated maple-walnut stock or a walnut stock, plus all the tricks used to make a solid match rifle."

I can't recommend Springfield enough.

A usual rifle assault course consists of firing a fixed number of shots at targets set at varying distances. Usually you fire, then advance to a new firing point, and fire again. It is Comstock-scored (time divided into points scored.) Matches like the *Soldier of Fortune* shoot require you to shoot prone, offhand, and through a window, and there's usually a mandatory reload in there somewhere.

Aside from the basic shooting skills, which will serve you very well here, you're going to have to learn how to speed-load a battle rifle. It works much the same as a .45 only the gun is a lot heavier. On the M1A/Mini-14 style gun, when the operating rod locks back, the weak hand should come off the forearm, hit the release and strip the old magazine off the gun, then go for a fully charged magazine in a weak-side pouch. The strong arm—and it has to be strong, too—holds up the rifle, ideally on the shoulder, while the new magazine is inserted. Remember that these rifles were meant for battle—they're not particularly fragile. Put the magazine in *hard* and make sure it seats solid. Practice this just like you would with a pistol, preferably with a magazine loaded with DUMMY bullets—they're easy to get for military calibers. Try reloading on the run and from a prone position.

An AR-15 is easier (and lighter). When you run out of rounds, the weak hand goes for the new magazine while the strong hand hits the magazine release button. Insert the magazine and trip the bolt release on the left side with the weak hand. You can do it quickly if you practice.

The magazines should fall out of the gun, which is a drawback with the H-K system, as is the fact that the bolt doesn't stay open on the final shot. You've also got to reach all the way forward and pull the bolt.

You should have one special magazine pouch that is strictly for speedloading. Most military magazine pouches do a good job, but they're usually made to keep the magazines securely in, not facilitate getting them out quickly. I have a leather pouch made by Gordon Davis, which holds the magazines securely and easily ac-

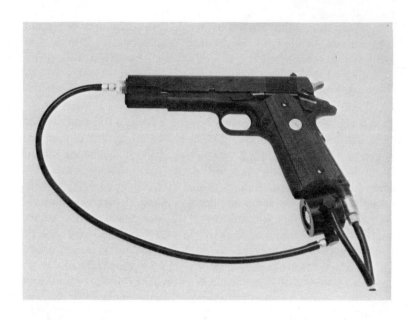

Advanced .45 Technology's FIRING SIMULATOR is the first breakthrough in dry fire practice that allows the .45 to be dry fired in a realistic manner as it cycles the slide, recoils, and cocks the hammer as fast as you can pull the trigger. Scores will be dramatically increased once practice is started using the FIRING SIMULATOR. Practice can begin anywhere, home or work, at a cost of less than 80 shots per penny when using CO_2.

The Advanced .45 Technology's FIRING SIMULATOR is a complete unit that requires no machining or modification to your .45 pistol. Easy drop in design includes recoil spring, air cylinder with adapter that replaces your barrel, and a new mainspring housing that exchanges with the original.

Two versions of the newest offering from Springfield Armory
— the M1A Combat, based on my rifle. Note the beefed-up
forend to give the bipod more support. In 1982, Springfield
now offers these rifles with built on rubber butt pads and
pistol grip full stock, in laminated walnut, called the Shaw
Combat Special. Muzzle Mizers are also available for these
rifles from Springfield. The first six places at Soldier of Fortune 1982 Rifle Match were won with heavy barrel M1As
designed after my rifle.

The Heckler and Koch HK-91 battle rifle, equipped with muzzle-mizer.

---

cessible.

How easy is practical rifle shooting?

At the 1981 *Soldier of Fortune* match, I ran into a really good shooter named Brian Enos, who's going to be a *power* in pistol shooting. I asked whether he was going to shoot the rifle match, and he said he'd be happy to except for a few minor things: He didn't own a battle rifle; had never shot a battle rifle. I said I'd loan him my rifle, if he needed it, and he agreed—if I'd throw in a couple of pointers before the match.

I'd zeroed the M1A that afternoon, and then I made a classic rookie mistake—as I went to the line to shoot, I raised the sight three clicks, which I felt certain it needed. I proceeded to shoot 21 head shots, which count only five points, as opposed to ten for body shots. I came off the line, turned the sights back three clicks, and gave the rifle to Brian.

"Front sight," I said. "Squeeze the trigger."

The timer buzzed before he'd gotten off his last shot, which cost him a "first" overall. As it was, he won about $5000 worth of prizes and knocked me from second place to third, which cost me about $1500. That's what friends are for, though.

It's a wide open sport, and one that's easy to get organized. You might want to appeal to the metallic silhouette shooters in your area who are ready for another challenge. It's also a sport that appeals—and helps—hunters.

Couple of quick tips, though. Stick to 20-round magazines. The others have a way of binding up every so often, which is once too many. Practice 100-yard offhand shooting, holding your groups to four or five inches. At 200 yards, practice getting into a prone position and getting off the shot quickly. That should take around three to four seconds. Try the same at 300 yards, and that should take you around five or six seconds.

The Combat Shotgun

There's probably more misinformation available on the shotgun than any other firearm. As I've said earlier, people tend to confuse shotguns with a magic cure for dangerous encounters—just point the gun in the general direction and let 'er rip, demolishing not only your target but trees, small houses, cars, anything else in the path. Maybe that's exaggerated, but the shotgun's reputation is built on its awesome ability to knock down anything in the path of the shot.

The shotgun's reputation is that of alley-clearer, just point and pull the trigger and something's *bound* to hit what you're aiming at. Well, that's just not so. Ask any dedicated bird hunter; it's more than just pointing and closing your eyes.

The idea of "practical" or "combat" shotgun shooting started out at Richard Davis's Second Chance bowling pin shoot a few years back. Originally, it was knocking ten bowling pins off the table at 25 feet with a 12-gauge. The fastest man won, and the speed eventually got down to around three-and-a-half seconds. Most of the people shooting started out with pumps, which are certainly the most common gun in America, considering the millions in the hands of police officers. A few people—including myself—started out with Remington automatics. The next year practically *everybody* had an automatic, the bulk being Remington 1100s.

The very first thing combat shotgunning did was demolish the cherished myth that, "a pump is just as fast as an automatic, in the right hands." The myth just didn't hold up under competition. We quickly discovered that the 1100 shotgun was great for competition and self-defense with two big "ifs" attached—you have to maintain it, and you have to have a shotgun that works to begin with. My 1100 hasn't malfunctioned in 2,000 rounds, and I probably trust it as much as my pump 870, because it's possible to short-shuck any pump and lock the whole thing up (more on that later). The main item that needs attention on the 1100 is the gas O-ring. Keep an eye on that, and the 1100 should last pretty much forever. I won the 1980 and 1981 Shotgun Championship at the Soldier of Fortune Shoot with an 1100—the first year with an 1100 I borrowed, since I didn't own one at the time.

On my original 1100, I've got four barrels: an Improved Cylinder for bowling pin shoots, a rifle-sighted barrel for the Second Chance slug match—that's shooting steel plates shaped like *tanks* at 40, 60, 80 and 100 yards; great fun—plus a couple of more conventional barrels. That gun has won the shotgun portion of Second Chance twice: I won in 1980, then I loaned the gun to another

133

One of the best exercises for the combat shotgunner is trap and skeet with your combat weapon.

shooter in 1981 and he beat me with it. I finished second.

The gun that I'm using this year is one that I won at Soldier of Fortune, donated by Garth Choate from Arkansas. I won an 1100 and an 870 pump, both with Choate's new pistol grip plastic stocks on them. I started using this 1100 for duck hunting and quail hunting, and I shot it better than any other shotgun I've ever used. The pistol grip is like an AR-15, at the same angle as a .45 automatic. It throws really well—most 1100s tend to throw their pattern very high; you've really got to get your cheek and eye down into the stock to bring it down. But the Choate stock solves all that. You bring it up, and you don't see anything but the bead, and that's what I like when I shoot a shotgun: just the bead—nothing of the barrel or the rib. The first time I took it out was duck hunting—I should probably mention it's got an 18-inch barrel and a Polychoke, (which I changed to a Winchoke screw-in choke) plus being Parkerized with a black plastic stock; did I ever get some laughs in the duck blind!—where I got one duck after another, the best I'd ever shot on ducks. People stopped laughing after the third duck. I screw in an improved choke to use it for bird hunting. The combination of stock, short barrel, and Winchoke was *deadly*. If I had to pick a shotgun for all seasons, that's got to be the one. I'm going to shoot my matches with it; I bird hunt with it; I duck hunt with it; I wouldn't hesitate to use it on deer—it's just a super gun.

I'm in the process of having a new barrel made for my 1100 that might prove even *more* versatile, though. Mark Duncan, an IPSC shooter and ace gunsmith in North Carolina, is working up a 24-inch ribbed barrel fitted with a Winchoke and a fold-down rifle sight fitted into the rib, similar to the shot barrel for the Thompson-Center Contender pistol. The advantage is having a slug sight without having to worry about having it knocked off when you're not using it.

"We can do it on any length barrel you want," Mark says. "Same with the Winchoke—I really think it's the coming thing. I've been able to get more consistent patterns out of the Winchoke than with a Polychoke."

Mark also specializes in revolver work, especially action jobs. He is, in fact, preparing my L-frame Smith and Wesson for the 1982 Bianchi Cup. I highly recommend his services.

I want to put in a word here for Garth Choate and his accessories. Choate's accessories *work*. His shotgun stocks and his extension magazines are the best in the business, and they go a long way toward bringing the shotgun into line as a combat weapon.

Just about everybody I know uses Choate's magazine extensions, which come in eight-, ten-, and 12-shot lengths. The reason Choate's tubes work so well is that they're all in one piece—most other extension tubes come in three pieces. Other brands tend to have a problem with the magazine spring and guide. If you tried to force an additional shell into the tube, the spring could bend in such a way as to prevent feeding. Choate uses a fiberglass plug and a spring guide to prevent that from happening. I've never had a jam with a Choate tube, and I've got four or five of them and shoot them extensively. A police department I work with bought Remington guns on my recommendation, but the guns came with Remington tubes. It didn't take long for the police armorer to call Choate looking for springs and followers. Same with a big national agency, which actually sent their production tubes to Choate to be welded into a single unit with Choate springs and followers added. Believe me, it's easier (and cheaper) just to buy the Choate tubes from the start. This is one item that I recommend 100 percent.

The new generation of Smith and Wesson riot guns will be coming with Choate tubes on their pumps as standard. I've shot the Smith and Wesson pump, and I really think it is good—maybe even better than the Remington 870. Smith has asked me to shoot one of their guns in competition, and I'm definitely looking forward to trying it. The one drawback to the S&W automatic will be that it's a five-shot only; its design precludes the use of an extension tube. What impressed me about S&W was their willingness to work with shooters to improve their products. It's been an open secret that S&W shotguns haven't found a lot of shooter acceptance in recent years. But S&W was willing to go back to the drawing board with the needs of the shooter, hunter and policeman in hand and come up with something new. My tendency is always to support the people who support the shooting sportsman.

Garth Choate, incidentally, has been one of my sponsors for some time, an association that I took on with pride. In fact, when I decided to add a shotgun training course to my school, the Mid-South Institute of Self-Defense Shooting, I went straight to Garth for his advice. We think the course—now called the Choate Shotgun Course—is one of the best available for that weapon.

To recap, if you want to get into practical shotgun shooting, or you feel better (as I do) with a scattergun around for personal defense, your first step is to obtain and outfit the proper gun. I don't see how you can go wrong with either the Remington 1100 or 870 or the *latest* generation of Smith and Wessons. Pass on any older Smiths.

Add the Choate stock and magazine tube for starters. As far as barrel lengths go. I had been shooting 26-inch modified before winning the 18-inch gun. Now, though, I'll have to give my wholehearted recommendation to the short gun with the Winchoke or Polychoke. Go ahead and let your friends laugh. They'll stop pretty quickly.

There are some things, however, that you definitely don't need.

One of these is a folding stock. It may make your 12-gauge look like the meanest pistol ever created, but when you unfold it and fire, you'll feel the lack of stock support throughout your shoulder and face! Remember, the essence of practical shooting and intelligent self-defense is aimed fired. It's hard to remember to aim that second shot when you're still trying to figure out what hit you. Whether you happen to be a gamesman or a martial artist, or whether you're trying to knock down ten bowling pins or save the life of your family, the object is to *win,* not prove how tough you are by taking unnecessary recoil.

Ironically, one of the much over-rated advantages of a folding stock shotgun is in hip-shooting. A folded stock *must* be better from the hip, right? While I can't speak for everyone, that certainly hasn't been the case with me. In fact, the best hip-shooting shotgun I own is the Choate-stocked 1100. The reason for that seems to be that when you hold the pistol grip and place the rest of the stock under your arm for better support, the gun is pointed in the same place every time. If you want to learn how to hip-shoot a shotgun, I think the Choate stock will help you 100 percent over a folding or a regular stock. Before you run out to start hip-shooting anything, consider that the same basic rules apply to hip-shooting a shotgun as apply to hip-shooting a pistol. In 99 percent of the situations you're likely to encounter either on a match course or in a self-defense situation, aimed fire is more effective. I and numerous other professional shooters have proved again and again that it only takes a fraction of a second to bring even a long gun to your shoulder and aim, and that an aimed shot is much more likely to achieve its purpose. This warning applies especially to police officers who shoot their riot guns only occasionally. If you've got to shoot it, aim it first!

There is a place for the folding stock, the purpose, in fact, for which the stock was originally designed. That is storing the gun in tight spaces, such as in a car, in a motor home, or on a boat, anyplace space is at a premium. Many folding stocks, I understand,

Speed-reloading the automatic shotgun as described in the text. It's really faster than it looks. Note the .45 magazine pouch used to hold the 12-gauge shells.

Reload with two shells — one in chamber/one in magazine.

Try shooting trap this way! The Choate stock lends itself to hip-shooting (top) and even works well in some unorthodox positions (below).

are being sold in South Florida to boat captains who'd like to discourage drug runners from "borrowing" their boats. Choate carries a line of folding stocks to meet these needs.

Another thing you'll want to pass on—with two exceptions—are rifle sights on a shotgun. Those two exceptions are shooting slugs at more than 60 yards in a match like Second Chance or in hunting with slugs. I still have mixed feelings about using rifle sights in hunting—if you're looking for 100-yard shots, you should use a rifle. The disadvantage to rifle sights is they get hung up on things during the use of the shotgun. Since they're not on there all that sturdily anyway, they tend to get knocked off, leaving you with no sights at all.

The same problem exists with slings and bandoleers to hold spare ammunition. On a defense gun, it's a good idea to have a reload on the gun, and the best way to accomplish this is with an elastic or lace-on holder on the stock. But in a match, or in a situation where speed loading counts for more than a few prizes, strap-on carriers or bandoleers are *no good.* They slow you down too much to use them. You have to fumble, with getting a new round out of the carrier; if it's on the stock or on the sling, you've got to take the gun down from your shoulder. For a match or for a real-life situation where firepower is going to spell the difference between life and death, it's hard to beat a shell bag on your hip—with all the shells arranged the same way. These bags carry plenty of ammunition, and it's easier to get to than any kind of bandoleer arrangement. As combat shotgunning becomes increasingly popular, I wouldn't be at all surprised to see a smart manufacturer come out with a "combat shell bag." I'm ready for it.

Think of slings the same way you think of folding stocks. How are you going to *use* your shotgun? For competition or home defense, you don't need a sling. You're running a risk of having the sling get tangled up on something like a bedpost or car door handle if you're not careful. The meat hunter who has to pack out the day's bag limit has the most obvious need for a sling.

What makes combat shotgunning different from any other use of the scattergun is the emphasis on hitting multiple targets in a short time span. This is a skill that even most police departments overlook. I once trained an elite S.W.A.T. team in handgunning, and after a tough day of pistol shooting, we turned to their issue pump shotguns. They'd all been bragging about how good the team was with shotguns, so I put up five targets at 15 yards, about one yard apart. The drill was to put one slug on each target in five

The proper use of a shotgun through a window. Note that neither the arm nor the gun touches the window at any point.

seconds—not a very tough drill, actually. Of the seven members of the team, only one member made it through without short-stroking his pump with all hits on the target. My time on the drill, using one of their terrible Winchester 1200 pumps, was 3.25 seconds with all hits in the nine-ring. Two cases of slugs later, most of the team could do it, too.

If you keep a pump shotgun for defense, remember that the pump must be worked *all the way*. A short stroke can lock the pump action up, leaving the shotgun useless.

There are a series of things necessary to get you and your shotgun ready for competition or effective self-defense. The first is to go bird hunting or skeet shooting. After spending a few days shooting fast-moving doves or skeet, those 18 X 24-inch metal targets—which aren't moving!—are going to look much easier to hit.

Pattern your shotgun barrel. Shotgun barrels are much more finicky than your grandfather led you to believe. I have full-choke guns that will act just like open choke with certain loads. The key thing here is to know for sure which load will produce the best pattern with a certain barrel. For competition, I use #00 buckshot, as do most of the other competitors, unless the course calls for slugs. For defense, I use and recommend #4 buck, and results of police shootings seem to back me up. Don't *ever* use 2¾-inch magnum buckshot in an 1100—it'll lock up the mechanism, as a lot of shooters unfortunately found out in recent matches.

Your basic exercise for combat shotgunning is engaging multiple targets. Start out with three targets at 15 yards and concentrate on good, solid hits. Your speed will come later. When you've got that down pat, add another target and pull back five yards. You might also want to take up trap and skeet, *using the same gun you plan to use in competition.*

Another important aspect of combat shotgunning is speed reloading. In a typical match you'll be running from position to position, and you'll be required to make a mandatory number of reloads. I recommend reloading on the run rather than waiting until you arrive at the new position and trying to reload two or three rounds all at once. *Always* carry two or three times as many rounds as you'll need—shotgun shells have a way of getting away from you quickly. It's easier to grab more than you need and let one drop rather than not having enough. If you're using a 12-gauge, a regular .45 magazine pouch is good for holding the next two rounds.

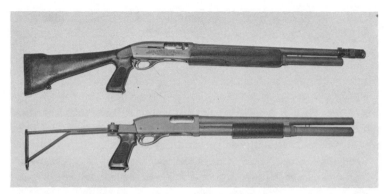

*Two shotguns that have **been** given **the full** Choate treatment:
top, my Remington 1100 with the 18-inch barrel, Polychoke
(recently replaced with a Winchoke), Parkerized finish and
Choate stock; bottom, a Remington 870 with a Choate
folding stock for use in tight places. Both feature the Choate
extension tube.*

If you're using a Remington 1100, the proper way to load two
rounds if the gun is locked open is to drop the first round directly
into the chamber, then trip the carrier release with the next round
as you're inserting it. The whole operation shouldn't take more
than three seconds from shot to shot. Same type operation with a
pump—pull the pump all the way back, drop a round into the
chamber, push the pump forward, then push second round into the
magazine tube. The same operation will take about a second longer
with a pump than an automatic. Try not to shoot it empty, though,
and just load into the magazine.

I confess that I'm partial to the shotgun. I never feel the tension before a shotgun match that I do before a pistol or rifle match.
But I believe that learning to use a shotgun properly is one of the
most useful firearm skills you can obtain. It will provide many happy hours in the game fields, and it could save your life one late
night.

I also highly recommend Ed Mason in Memphis for installing
the Winchoke System on your shotguns. Ed is an Olympic Gold
medalist with muzzle loading shotguns and knows his business with
shotgun barrels. I recommend cutting the barrel off no shorter than
21 " or longer than than 24 ". There is a possibility the barrel will split
when it is expanded to except the Winchoke, so one should start with
the 24 " and just in case it does split, then you can go to the 21 ".

So Called Gadget Guns

The 1980 IPSC Nationals seem to have started a revolution in competitive combat guns. I won the 1980 Nationals with a Jim Clark "pin-gun," the only one of its kind in the competition. I also won the 1981 Nationals with the same gun, but there were four other "pin-guns" in the competition with all five finishing in the top sixteen places. In 1982, nineteen of the top twenty shooters used some type of heavy-barrel .45 Automatic. Shooters and their gunsmiths seem to be in a race to produce a .45 with reduced recoil that is reliable and accurate, and still falls within a reasonable price range. Jim Clark, Bill Wilson, Mike Plaxco, Guy Hammond and Eddie Brown are building many of the heavy-barrel .45's being used today.

Since I have been shooting a heavy-barrel .45 longer and more successfully than any other competitor to date, I feel I can give an accurate report on the progress of the heavy-barrel .45. I own at least one gun built by each of the above mentioned gunsmiths. When looking at each gun in regards to weight, accuracy, reliability, recoil control and price, they all compare very favorably.

Before we discuss the different characteristics of a heavy-barrel .45, let's define a "pin-gun." The "pin-gun" was invented by Jim Clark for use in bowling pin matches such as Second Chance. There was a need for a gun that could handle the hot loads in rapid succession with reduced recoil. Mr. Clark's idea was to add weight to the barrel, rather than the slide. All the mentioned gunsmiths use some variation of this idea to produce low-recoil .45's, thus they are all referred to as "pin-guns."

Maxi-Comp by Ed Brown. This is a gun I'm highly impressed with. Recoil is low, accuracy is good, price and delivery are reasonable. A super gun for all occasions.

Added weight to the barrel is the most important aspect of recoil reduction. The barrel used itself weighs anywhere from 3 oz. to 7 oz. more than the regular five inch .45 barrel. It is important that this added weight be kept on the front of the gun and not slamming back at you in the form of a heavier slide.

For years, gunsmiths have been building five or six inch slides with ribs attached for added weight to reduce recoil. True, the recoil is not as sharp, but the movement of the gun is about the same as the standard five inch gun. Basically, the heavy slide reduces the cycle time of the weapon creating a "gluck-gluck" feeling as the slide comes back and goes forward. The weight of the slide does cushion the blow to your hand as the slide comes back, but it also causes the muzzle to dip as it goes forward to the slide stop, making a rapid succession of well placed shots difficult. All of the gunsmiths I've mentioned are now building their guns on Commander slides to further reduce slide weight.

So we see that the weight should be added to the front of the barrel, rather than to the slide. How much weight can be added to the barrel and not become too heavy for practical competitive shooting? The gun built by Ed Brown weighs 2 lbs. 10 oz., which I think is the upper limit in weight. Mike Plaxco's guns weigh 2 lbs. 7 oz., which is the lightest built, and I think the lower limit for the weight category. I think guns within these weight limits are practical and can be suited to individual needs and weight preferences.

The length of the barrel past the end of the slide should be no longer than 1½ inches and no shorter than 1 inch. Clark, Brown, Hammond and Plaxco use 6 inch match-grade barrels made by Jim Clark. Bill Wilson uses a 5 inch barrel. Their systems for adding their weights vary. Brown and Plaxco use a standard bushing in their guns with their compensator screwed onto the end of the barrel that protrudes past the slide. Clark, Hammond and Wilson use a threaded cone-shaped sleeve that screws on the barrel all the way back to the lugs creating a lock-up between the end of the slide and the widest cone area.

Porting also has an effect on recoil. Porting is the cutting of small vents in the top end of the extended barrel which forces gas pressure up as bullet exits, holding the muzzle down. Brown and Plaxco guns come ported as standard equipment. Wilson, Clark and Hammond leave this option to the shooter ordering the gun. Porting definitely reduces gun movement. A Wilson or Clark gun that is not ported will kick up 9 inches from line of sight as compared to 7 inches when shooting a ported Wilson or Clark gun using hardball equivalent loads. Two inches per shot is quite a difference when eight shots are fired in rapid succession.

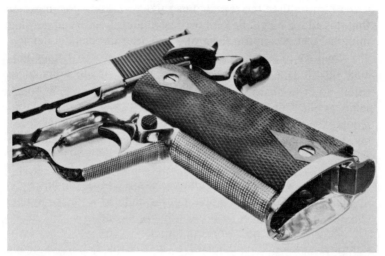

Alpha Precision Inc. owned by Jim Stroh offers the finest reloading modification on the market. The metal is welded to the frame of the gun then precisely pressed down to the contour of the factory grips on the outside. Beveled and polished on the inside. The opening is 150% greater than the original and magazine change time is reduced by one third. His checkering is also some of the best available.

In regards to accuracy, a "pin-gun" should shoot under 4 inch groups at 50 yards. I have found through experience that porting may greatly effect the accuracy and velocity of your gun. My Clark gun shot 2½ at 50 yards before I ported it and 3½ inches after it was ported. I have seen 2 inch groups open up to 4 inch groups after porting. We tested one gun with a screw-on compensator. Before the compensator was installed, it shot 2½ inch groups out of a Ransom Rest at 50 yards. We left the gun in the rest, installed a compensator, shot the same ammo and had 8½ inch groups. We installed another compensator and got 3½ inch groups. We can easily see the variations you can get and the experimentation necessary to get your gun within acceptable accuracy limits.

So there is a compromise between recoil reduction and accuracy. Personally, I'll give up 1 to 1½ inches at 50 yards to get the recoil reduction necessary for rapid succession firing, but I definitely would not give up any more than that.

Many people are calling "pin-guns" gadgetry or Star Wars

specials and are pushing to have them removed from competition. Anyone who has used a "pin-gun" can definitely see the advantages of the reduced recoil and longer sight radius in sport competition. I certainly prefer to have these added advantages when shooting for large cash stakes, national titles or personal defense.

Contrary to popular belief, these are not strictly competition guns. I trust my main competition guns more than any other guns I own. This includes pistols, rifles and shot guns. The reason being, I shoot these guns thousands of rounds more than any other guns I own with zero malfunctions. Think about it. If you carry a gun which you have shot maybe 500 to 1000 rounds total with just one jam, or say no jams at all, is it more reliable than one you shoot two or three times a week for a total of 20,000 rounds a year without a single malfunction. One can see the obvious choice.

The only alterations I would not recommend would be a super light trigger or a trigger stop on a duty gun due to an accidental discharge or trigger stop working loose.

Maybe in the future there will be a place for both conventional and special guns in sports competition without producing any controversy.

Another gunsmith that does a super light trigger job and can make a .45 reliable is Ed Pitt of "The Gun Room" in Smyrna, Georgia. Ed does trigger jobs for a lot of top competitors in the sport. So if you need a trigger job or some work to make your .45 more functionable and do not want to wait, Ed Pitt is the man to **contact.**

"Shaw's Pro Shooters Bag" (Made by Eagle Industries)
A necessary convenience for all shooters. It has eight different compartments for ammo, magazines, leather, stop watch, etc. It also has 2 removable padded zipper pistol pouches. The bag has a 300 pound test weight with carrying strap.

What Was New In '82

Practical shooters are part of the fastest growing sport in America. The 1982 shooting year saw many steps forward, such as more sponsors, bigger match purses — with one glaring exception — new products and better media coverage, giving, in general, a clearer picture of the shooting sports.

In this chapter I'd like to trace the 1982 shooting year, including match winners, their ideals, my recollection of events and a discussion of products and their effect on the sport.

The year started off with Mike Plaxco winning the Steel Challenge match in California; he went on to win the IPSC Nationals in Moline, Illinois., later in the year. Mickey Fowler, as usual, won the 1982 Bianchi Cup — his third win there — winning a record amount of prizes, totaling $35,000. Bill Wilson won the Second Chance Combat Match for the second time. Finally, I won the 1982 Soldier of Fortune Three-Gun-Match for the second time in three years, with a total purse of $10,000, second only to the Bianchi Cup.

I must say that this didn't seem to be a good year for me in the sport. I started the year off opening my school, the Mid-South Institute for Self Defense Shooting (MISS), and working on the first edition of YOU CAN'T MISS, and that seemed to add a great deal of pressure on me as a shooter. I found myself worrying about winning matches to help the book sell or to boost the school. As a result, I didn't shoot well at all in the matches.

Sure enough, the results of that added pressure was evident. In the first major match of the year, the Steel Challenge, I placed ninth. The year before, I had won it. I was tenth at the Bianchi Cup, tenth at Second Chance. At Second Chance, my five-pin score was better than the winning score of 1981, but it wasn't good enough. I shot conservatively, making sure of every shoot, and, consequently, I didn't shoot fast enough.

About the fourth day of the match, I was seven places down and sinking every day. Some people who were virtually new to the sport were ahead of me. I was eating lunch the fourth day, and Bill Wilson happened to drop by. I asked him what was going on. I was ½ second faster on my time the year before, and I was still seven places behind the leader. He said he didn't know either, except he felt like there were a lot more serious shooters in 1982 than ever before.

Keeping in mind the fast times that had already been turned in, I asked Bill how he was going to shoot this match.

He looked at me and said, "John, I'm going to be first place or last place. I don't care about second."

One hour later he shot the fastest time at Second Chance ever recorded in the five-pin event. He was dead serious about shooting, as evidenced by the fact that he emptied his gun on three of the five tables knocking the pins off. I practice with Bill, and he's every bit as good a pistol shot as I am, although he's never won any of the big matches except Second Chance — which is no small feat! It all boils down to nerves on race day. He did the best he could do, and he came out a winner. Holding back has cost him — and myself, I realized — matches in the past.

However, holding back now and trying to shoot conservative will get you beat. There you go beating yourself again! I went on to win other events and even set other records at Second Chance, always keeping in mind what Bill had told me — did I want to go all out to win, or did I want to shoot conservatively and let the other shooters make the mistakes? Bill had shown me the way.

I went into the IPSC Nationals with a bad mental attitude — I'd broken my right arm seven weeks before, and my thoughts were grim. I'd had my arm in a cast and, not surprisingly, there hadn't been much time to practice. The result? Zero confidence.

I started off shooting conservatively, trying not to make any mistakes. I missed a stop plate four times on the first day, plus nicking a hostage the second day. The more conservatively I shot, the further behind I got. Not counting how bad I felt as that of being a yearling rookie again.

I could have shot the rest of the match solid and probably finished around fourth or fifth, but I remembered what Bill told me. Nobody remembers who finishes second or third — they only remember who wins. I came out there to do my best, and doing my best meant going for it. I'm not saying that second place isn't something to be proud of, if you yourself know that's the very best you can do. But a second place for someone who's held back his performance and knows it, second is not a reward. That's exactly what I thought about myself.

The last day of the nationals we had two long assault courses to run, and I thought to myself, "I'm going to be first or last on these two matches." I wasn't holding back anything. The first match was the Superman Boogie. I set up to shoot through a barrel the wrong way and had to try and make up time on the stop plate. I missed my first two shoots and finally nicked it on the third. I finished 17th. The next match was a modified Cooper Assault. I had a gun malfunction, and, once again, trying to make time up, I knocked over a bar that added ten seconds to my time. I finished 19th at the U.S. Nationals, a big come-down from winning it the two previous years. In fact, that's the lowest I've ever finished in the five major matches. But I was more satisfied with myself for

150

going out there on the last day and giving it 100 percent, not caring where I finished. It was a great relief to go out there and do my best, without caring who was watching, what it would mean to my career, or how much I could win. My sponsors I have now told me, win loose or draw, they were still behind me.

Going to the next match, the Soldier of Fortune Match, I had the same attitude I had the last day of the Nationals. I went to win, or go home last or close to it. I went into that match knowing that if I really went for it, I'd be hard to beat.

In fact, Garth Choate, one of the main sponsors of the match, asked me about a month before I went if I thought I was going to win. I told him if my guns worked, I would win. So he showed up at the match with the first place trophy with my name already engraved on it!

Talk about pressure! I told him I sure wish he hadn't done that, but I wasn't going to think about it anymore. I shot those matches the best I could do, and I won first place with a 99 percent score. My closest competitor, Bill Rogers, finished with a 91 percent.

It was by far my most satisfying win. I did the best I could do to satisfy myself, and I won the match.

What's Happening In The Sport

The big news in 1982 for the professional shooter was larger prizes and more money in the matches, with, as I said before, one major exception. The IPSC National's purse this year was the biggest let-down the sport has had in five years.

This year's second place was a Colt Gold Cup Pistol. Sixth place was a Bar-Sto barrel; 14th place was a $37 B-B gun; 17th place was a folding Buck knife. The sponsoring body took in over $67,000 in entrance fees for this match — a $125 entrance fee, plus 75 percent of each club's mission count, which was $100 a head for each shooter sent. Sixty thousand dollars was given to the Milan Gun Club. Of that sum, a very large portion of that money was spent on improving the club's own range and a sizeable amount was spent on a banquet meal which consisted of a nonelaborate buffet dinner for the shooters. Five months after the 1982 Nationals, no itemized financial statement has been made available to shooters or IPSC clubs.

To spend large amounts of IPSC dollars on a borrowed range is a questionable investment instead of buying nicer prizes. All the prizes were donated from sponsors. It was, I believe, the least prizes ever given out in a National IPSC Championship.

For example, Bill Wilson finished 14th in 1982 and got a $37 B-B gun; he finished 14th in 1977 and got a $150 spotting scope. In 1981, the first ten places practically got their ways paid for through the prizes. This year, if you didn't win first place, you didn't even break even on the match. Figuring it cost everybody at least $1,000 by the time you included airfare, hotels and meals, the second place finisher lost about $600.

These were also the largest entry fees ever paid, taking in much more money than the Bianchi Cup, where the prizes were phenomenal.

Yes, it sounds mercenary, but consider this:

This is exactly what killed bullseye and PPC shooting.

The reason practical shooting has been growing by leaps and bounds is because of the prizes. Some of the top bullseye and PPC shooters in the country have shifted over to combat competition because of the prizes. That is the bottom line.

One thing I'd like to see back in 1983 is metal targets. The IPSC banned metal targets for local competition in 1982, which was, I feel, another short-sighted move. Metal targets have tremendous spectator appeal — look at the Bianchi Cup or the Steel Challenge. Plus, metal targets are fun to shoot, and they help bring shooters into the sport. Finally, they're challenging — raise your head once on a plate match and you've missed.

Ironically, the Nationals used metal stop plates in five of the six matches, and the last-day shoot-off was all on metal! If the IPSC rules were strictly followed, some shooters might make the Nationals without ever having shot on metal targets, finding themselves at a super disadvantage.

The 1982 Nationals represents a major turn in the wrong direction. It is not my intention to cast a gloomy shadow on IPSC matches, rather I am 100% behind supporting IPSC and its goals. I have and will continue to offer my help in the future despite any controversy.

This shooting sport has a strong potential to appeal both to the professional shooter who expects and needs good prizes and substantial cash purses in return to continue his large investment in the sport. Plus, there is adequate room for the shooter who prefers matches to enable him to meet his own expectations in a street encounter with little emphasis on rewards or prizes.

I hope in 1983 to see better management of funds, more reactionary targets and most important a democratic, respectful decision making body at the leadership of IPSC. This would in return get more shooters and more sponsors interested in the sport and supporting it unconditionally.

Ironically, this was also the year that the shooting sports began getting television coverage on such shows as *Look At Us* and *20-20*. I have been on talk shows discussing shooting and the shooting sports. We've gotten some straight press coverage, including a pro-gun — probably the first pro-gun — article in a men's magazine, *Oui*. The National Rifle Association jumped into the practical shooting arena at the 1982 Bianchi Cup, and that match became the first NRA-sanctioned practical match. The NRA has held a number of practical matches. In fact, I won the first open-to-the-public practical match in Atlanta mid-year.

Federal law enforcement, the police and even the military are recognizing the value of IPSC-type shooting in law enforcement. I predict in the next three or four years we're going to see wholesale support of IPSC style shooting by these agencies. And I predict that it's going to trickle down to police officers, who are going to be embarrassed to see something like the Bianchi Cup on television and realize how fast and accurate civilians can shoot. I think it's going to prompt their interest in combat shooting.

There were more sponsors for the shooting sports than ever before. The Bianchi Leather Company, as usual in the forefront, has offered a "$40,000 Proposition." Competitors in the six major matches can earn $120 just by wearing a Bianchi holster, and stand to win as much as $1000 for winning the match.

I can't speak highly enough of John Bianchi. He's turned the Bianchi Cup into the crown jewel of pistol shooting, and he's thrown his company wholeheartedly behind practical shooting. With more people like him, the shooting sports will achieve the recognition it so amply deserves.

A couple of other promising signs appeared in 1982. There are more women and teenagers than ever before in the sport, and more shooters are excelling without having to quit their jobs and shoot full-time. It proves you can be a champion in this sport without creating a hardship for a shooter in his job.

In fact, I think there's a whole new image of the practical shooter. You sure can't call Mickey Fowler a "gun-nut," for winning $35,000 in one match and doing as a hobby. We're setting the pace for law enforcement of the future. Mickey is now doing a column for the *American Handgunner,* Ross Seyfried is writing for *Guns & Ammo Magazine*, and I have written several articles along these same lines in various gun magazines.

We've also seen the rise of the Aimpoint sight, and I think most of the serious competitors this year will be sporting the electronic sights in the Bianchi Cup. I predict a Bianchi win with an Aimpoint.

"Shaw Challenger"

Last year, I was privileged to work with several sponsors on a number of shooter-oriented projects. Springfield Armory has began shipping the "John Shaw Combat Special," an M1A set up for combat competition with a laminated walnut pistol grip stock, rubber built plate and Harris Bipod. I now use a strong side forward tilt holster with a cut down front.

Bill Rogers has done it again! Just what I recommended to be done. A shell pouch you can draw two shells from every time, instead of one at a time.

George Whipple, my friend at Atlanta Arms and Ammo, has come out with an excellent lead bullet for the shooter of all disciplines, labeled the "Shaw Bullet." It is a more rounded shaped H&G style bullet. I believe this is probably the most accurate lead bullet on the market. I also worked with Eagle Industries on the "Shaw Pro Shooters" bag which is suitable for any type shooter. It features two padded, zipper cases for your pistols plus compartments for ammo, headphones, and leather. With a 300 pound test weight material it will not tear. One of the best products ever made for the shooter. Used by most of the top shooters in the country.

154

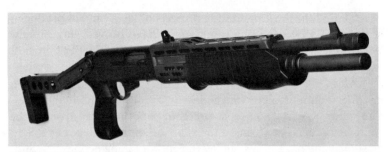

SPAS-12 shotgun by Franchi is the newest of combat autos. I was really impressed with this gun having shot over 1,000 rounds through it at Weapons Expo in Los Angeles this year without a malfunction. It can be used as an auto or pump, comes with adjustable choke tubes, extended magazine, folding pistol grip and with a full stock that's going to be offered. A real good weapon.

Two great new shotguns were released last year, one of the most interesting shotguns ever invented is the SPAS-12 distributed by Franchi. It's both an auto and a pump, it looks like a M60 and it works and keeps on working, my only complaint is the folding stock although a solid pistol grip stock is in the making.

Mossberg is offering a new auto with adjustable chokes, similar to the Winchoke that seems to be promising. Both these shotguns should give the 1100 a run for its money in 1983.

*Now for MINI-14 Harris Bipod and adapter. Fits standard and ranch models. Will not fit **Ruger** folding stock model. The adapter is quick detachable and accommodates **Harris** LR Bipod.*

One of the most interesting projects of last year was producing a series of video training tapes which have proved very popular with both civilans and police departments. I offer these in both pistol and shotguns.

All in all, it was a good year for the shooting sports. For me, my MISS school is a growing endeavor, and I welcome all inquiries. The more people we have in practical shooting, the stronger the sport becomes. The stronger the sport becomes, the harder it is to blast the handgun as "just an instrument for killing people," as anti-gunners are fond of doing. High visibility is important to all of us.

Good shooting!

Suppliers

Listed below are the suppliers mentioned in "You Can't Miss." These companies and individuals have shown a willingness to work with shooters and to support the shooting sports, and I recommend them highly. If you should contact them, please mention that you saw them listed in "You Can't Miss."

1. Advanced .45 Technology
1031 Elder St. JS
Oxnard, California 93030
(805) 485-0113
(805) 485-4435
The Firing Simulator is a very effective and inexpensive way for you to practice at home for self-defense or recreation."
2. Atlanta Arms and Ammo
6721 Covington Highway
Lithonia, Georgia 30358
(404) 987-2142
Top-quality reloads at a reasonable price from Atlanta Arms. There is none better.
3. Brown's Gun Shop - J.S.
Route 1, Box 153
Perry, Missouri 63462
(314) 565-3261
Ed Brown is a newcomer to building combat pistols. Inventor of the Maxi-Comp which is a super system for accuracy and recoil reduction. A real nice fellow to do business with.

4. Choate Machine and Tool Company
Garth Choate, owner
P.O. Box 218
Bald Knob, Arkansas 72010
(501) 724-3138
His selection of custom stocks, shotgun extension tubes, and other accessories is a must for the serous shooter. Write for a catalog.

5. Clark Custom Guns
Jim Clark, gunsmith
Route 2, Box 22A
Keithville, Louisiana 71047
(318) 925-0836
You can't miss dealing with Jim Clark. His target handguns have won every major competition in the country, and I feel that his Bowling Pin Gun is the single best choice for IPSC competition shooting.

6. Competition Electronics
753 Candy Lane
Rockford, Illinois 61111
(815) 654-3455
A super timer - I use it every time I practice.

7. Dillon Precision Reloaders
Mike Dillon, president
7755 East Gelding Dr.
Suite 106
Scottsdale, Arizona 85260
(602) 948-8009
The best progressive reloaders on the market are from Dillon.

8. Eagle Industries (Assault Cases)
55 Lincoln
St. Louis, Missouri 63119
(314) 968-4144
One of my longest sponsors, Eagle Industries makes a full time of assault cases, including one I helped design especially for combat handgunners. There's nothing like them on the market, especially at the price.

9. Harris Engineering, Inc.
Barlow, Kentucky 42024
(502) 334-3633
Harris bipods were on the top six rifle shooters guns in the 1982 Soldier of Fortune match. These bipods are a great help on hunting, combat or long range pistols. The best on the market.

10. Gil Hebard Guns

Specialist in handguns and shooting supplies
125-129 Public Square
Knoxville, Illinois 61448
There is no substitute for competitive experience when it comes to best serving the needs of the pistol shooter. Gil Hebard has done it all from being a national record holder to the "Top Ten Outstanding American Handgunner Award." He handles products for pistol shooters of all disciplines. Write for free catalog.

11. Hornady Manufacturing

P.O. Box 1848
Grand Island, Nebraska 68801
(308) 382-1390
Hornady needs no introduction—a bulletmaker attuned to the needs of shooters. Hornady bullets have won two IPSC National Championships, the World IPSC Championship, Soldier of Fortune Pistol and Rifle Match, the Bianchi Cup, and the Steel Challenge.

12. Ed Mason (Gunsmith)

5116 Park
Memphis, Tennessee 38117
(901) 767-8674
For any of your shotgun needs Ed can do it. He is also making up heavy barrel mini 14's that shoot exceptionally well.

13. Metaloy Industries, Inc.

Lee Cole & Bill Wilson, owners
Rt. 3, Box 211-D
Berryville, Arkansas 72616
(501) 545-3611
Metaloy Gun Plating: Metaloy is a hard chrome electroplating process which produces extreme hardness, friction reduction, and corrosion resistance. It will not chip, flake, crack, peel or separate. New owners, Lee Cole and Bill Wilson are committed to provide a product with the quality of excellence. Metaloy is the choice of champions Lee Cole, Brian Enns, Rob Leatham, John Shaw and Bill Wilson. For information write Metaloy Industries, Inc. at the above address.

14. Nite-Site

Julio Santiago, marketing
P.O. Box "O"
Rosemount, Minnesota 55068
Santiago offers a radium night sights for handguns, shotguns, and rifles.

15. Rogers' Holsters
Bill Rogers, owner
1736 St. Johns Bluff Road
Jacksonville, Florida 32216
Bill Rogers makes excellent holsters, .45 bullets (H&G#68), gadgets such as the Rogers funnel, the Shok-Buff (a Rogers/Bill Wilson creation), and the excellent Rogers/Wilson combat magazine.

16. Springfield Armory
Dennis Reese, president
420 West Main
Genesco, Illinois 61254
(309) 944-3122
Springfield is the maker of the M1A and the Garand.

17. Jim Stroh
Alpha Precision, Inc.
1231 Sunderland Ct.
Atlanta, Georgia 30319
(404) 458-0477
Does gunsmith work of all types plus makes the best mag well in the business.

18. Wilson's Gun Shop
Bill Wilson, gunsmith
Rt. 3, Box 211-D
Berryville, Arkansas 72616
(501) 545-3618
Gunsmith and IPSC shooter Bill Wilson's catalog is available for $2.00.

19. Wichita Arm Inc.
444 Ellis
P.O. Box 1171
Wichita, Kansas 67211
(316) 265-0661
Makes a great adjustable sight for your .45 auto plus other accessories. Their new sight with stainless steel leaf is guaranteed 200,000 rounds. Super warranty for the best sight on the market.

If you're interested in learning more about or enrolling in John Shaw's **M**id-**S**outh **I**nstitute of **S**elf-**D**efense **S**hooting, or wish to order any of the products listed below, please use this convenient coupon.

☐ Please send me information and class schedules for the **M**id-**S**outh **I**nstitute of **S**elf-**D**efense **S**hooting.

☐ Please send me _____ additional copies of "You Can't Miss," (3rd Edition) at $9.95 each, plus $1.00 each postage and handling.

☐ Shaw Pro's Shooters Bag, $69.95 (Black or Tan)

☐ Advance Firing Simulation, $120.00

☐ Beta or VHS Pistol Training Tape, $59.95

☐ Beta or VHS Shotgun Training Tape, $49.95

☐ Shaw Speed•E•Load, $29.95

Name _____

Address _____

City _____

State _____ Zip _____

Amount enclosed $ _____

MAIL TO:
Mid-South Institute
of Self-Defense Shooting
503 Stonewall
Memphis, Tennessee 38112